POTS, PANS
& Peace

The Legacy of Margaret Corey

By
Eleanor Corey

ALSO BY ELEANOR COREY

Sticks, Stones & Songs—The Corey Story

Pots, Pans & Peace:
The Legacy of Margaret Corey

Edit: David Jacobsen
Proofreading: Shelby Zacharias
Cover design: Elizabeth Dolhanyk
ISBN for paperback: 978-1-7340358-0-3

Library of Congress Control Number: 2019917576

1. Corey, Guderian, Eleanor. 2. Biography—woman of faith.
3. Rural family—farm work, hardship.
4. History—Olympic Peninsula, Washington.
5. Victory—peace, hope, humor. 6. Ministry—service, prayer.
7. Great Depression.

You may contact the author at
Eleanor Corey Guderian
eleanor@eleanorcorey.com
or
PO Box 571 Stanwood WA 98292

"Now has come the time, Margaret and Arthur, to evaluate what has occurred in your lives...and it's been a lot."

—*M. LaVerne Baker, 1979*

POTS, PANS & PEACE
The Legacy of Margaret Corey

is dedicated
to those who cherished Margaret Corey in her lifetime
and to those who will come to appreciate her pilgrimage of faith
through the words in this book.

TABLE OF CONTENTS

LIST OF PHOTOS

FOREWORD
By J. Allen Thompson

To Eleanor Corey Guderian we give an armload of kudos for writing this remarkable true story of her mother's pilgrimage. Margaret Corey came from a close-knit extended family of aunts and uncles, and engaged with a social religious community in the prestigious Presbyterian Church in Tacoma. She was little prepared to raise children, often by herself, in the rough and tumble of a logging community in the Olympic Peninsula.

In *Pots, Pans and Peace*, Eleanor organized hundreds of pages from her mother's writings into themes that vibrate with energy, and she certified the origin of facts in Author End Notes. Her choice of the book's title appropriately reflects the ordinariness of life where God in mercy reaches us and gives the peace he promises.

We read memoirs to put ourselves in another's shoes and to discover issues and motives that will strengthen our own. Margaret Corey's self-sacrifice—through serving her family and honoring her God in the depression era of the 1900s—hardly seems believable in today's secular and self-centered age. Will we be put off by Margaret's willingness to endure hardship in the midst of uncertainty, to remain steadfast in faith with empty cupboards and hungry children, and to refrain from paralyzing complaints?

Regardless of our circumstances today, the Christian path Margaret followed boils down to three disciplines: trust, prayer, and obedience. Look at her life. See how she continually committed herself to Christ. For 60-plus years—from her twenties to her eighties—she cherished, toiled, laughed, worried, believed, agonized, failed, matured, and triumphed. You won't remain unmoved.

---J. Allen Thompson, PhD
Mission Strategist and Retired CEO of World Team

PREFACE

Following the publication of my first book—*Sticks, Stones &
Songs: The Corey Story*—I sensed that Margaret, my mother, had
more to say about our shared history. So I mined once again her
fifty-some years of archives, uncovering also—in her trove of
treasures—the prodigious memoirs of my father, Arthur. Rising
from my semi-retirement chair, I began to sketch a biography that
logic argued Margaret herself should narrate. As the scribe,
however, I have taken liberty to wordsmith her entries for your
comprehension and enjoyment.

Margaret and Arthur are no longer with us to provide their
interpretation, so my siblings have searched their own recollections
and confirmed...or added to...the facts—at least as precisely as
their memories have permitted. I thank them for helping me give
voice to Margaret Corey through *Pots, Pans & Peace*.

Eleanor Corey Guderian and Margaret Corey, 1986

NORTHWEST WASHINGTON MAP

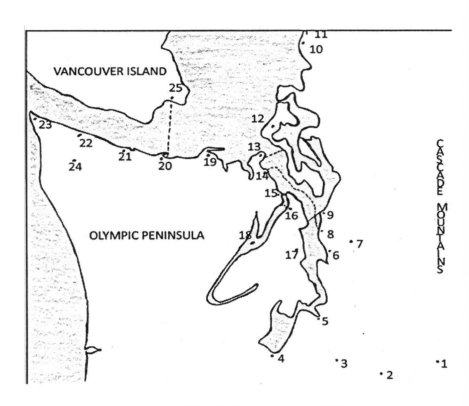

1 Mount Rainier	10 Bellingham	19 Sequim
2 Hart's Lake	11 To BC, Canada	20 Port Angeles
3 Roy/McKenna	12 Whidbey Island	21 Joyce/
4 Olympia	13 Port Townsend	Crescent Beach
5 Tacoma	14 Port Ludlow	22 Clallam Bay
6 Seattle	15 Hood Canal Bridge	23 Neah Bay
7 Bellevue	16 Lofall	24 Forks
8 Ballard	17 Bremerton	25 Victoria, BC
9 Edmonds	18 Hood Canal	

THE COREY FAMILY
1987

Arthur Wheelock Corey (b. 1904)

Margaret Lenore Phenicie Corey (b. 1905)

Virginia Corey McLennan (b. 1930) married to *John McLennan.*

Marilyn Corey Thompson (b. 1932) married to *Allen Thompson.*

Elizabeth Corey Richardson (b. 1934) married to *Bill Richardson.*

David Corey (b. 1937) married to *Violet (Vi) Traina Corey.*

John Corey (b. 1940) married to *Jeanette Hawkinson Corey.*

Phillip Corey (b. 1942) married to *Darlene Howell Corey.*

Eleanor Corey Guderian (b. 1943) married to *Ron Guderian.*

Merton Corey (b. 1945) married to *Debra Thompson Corey.*

Marian Corey Alwine (b. 1947) married to *Dennis Alwine.*

Janice Corey Lewis (b. 1952) married to *Dave Lewis.*

Corey Family Photo, 1989
Back row: Janice, Marian, Arthur, Merton*, Eleanor
Front row: Phillip, John, David, Margaret, Elizabeth, Marilyn, Virginia
*Merton recovering from logging accident

--PROLOGUE--

Not my time yet

January 20, 1987. Almost two months have gone by, but dates have not much meaning. I have been at death's door—so they tell me. *(The diary)*

A s I, Margaret Phenicie Corey, scribbled these words in my diary, I considered how abruptly the order of life can be thrown out of whack. My previous entry—two months earlier, on November 15, 1986—told of an unproductive elk-hunting trip and the gathering of twenty cousins, aunts, and uncles to celebrate the eighth birthday of my granddaughter, Janell. I also noted that during the festivities my wrists were sore and my entire body felt out-of-sorts.

Then I encountered a page full of snow-white silence.

Slowly I began to grasp what had happened during those two months of illness. The discomfort I'd felt in my joints had progressed to fever, dehydration, and incoherence. All night my daughter Eleanor drizzled water into my mouth and placed cold packs on my head. In the morning her medical-missionary husband, Ron Guderian, helped medics load me onto a mattress in the back of a van. They rushed me from our home near Joyce, Washington, to the hospital in Port Angeles—about 13 miles—where I was stuck for several hours in an admittance room. Eleanor said Arthur (my husband of 58 years) paced the floor, his face flushed and his hands raised to God, while she sat with me—praying the IV fluids would keep the blood flowing in my veins until a room was available. "Thankfully, God answered," she declared. "He still has work for you to do, and we still need you."

Calls to share news of my close encounter with eternity were made to our distant families: John and Jeanette in Liberia, West Africa; Phil and Darlene in the Dominican Republic; Virginia and John in Texas; and Marilyn and Allen in Georgia. The US-based couples caught flights to join the rest of the gathered family, which included Eleanor and Ron on furlough from Ecuador, South America, and the locals: Elizabeth and Bill, David and Vi, Merton and Debbie, Marian and Dennis, and Janice and Dave.

After the fact, my daughters—I have six of them, in case you've lost count—explained the sequence of happenings during their round-the-clock vigils in my hospital room. They explained how I was hooked up with tubes that were plugged into machines; how they waited and watched and conferred with all who entered their presence; and how they interpreted for Arthur, sending him home each evening with their belief I was improving. Which I was. For as soon as my wobbly legs could hold my weight, the girls switched to cheering and pushing and prodding—never letting up, they said—until I was strong enough for Arthur to chauffeur me home.

Where was I during those weeks lost from the calendar? I don't recall white tunnels or flashbacks of my life, and I can only conjure up those hospital images as they were portrayed to me by those who were there.

My vision of the first days at home is also muddled and murky. But recollections were rebuilding. I drank the *healthy* concoctions made by my daughters whether I wanted to or not. I basked in the punctiliousness of Marilyn whose special gift is caring for people in dire conditions—that's where I was—and the aroma of soapy water she used to scour the house. The cogs of my memory revolved a bit faster each day as Virginia played the piano and the girls sang my favorite hymns. The verses from Scripture Arthur read to me revitalized my comprehension of God's Word, and his prayers for my restoration strengthened my spirit.

Eleanor cooked turkey for Christmas and turned the leftovers into a couple dozen frozen TV dinners we could pull out after she and family returned to Ecuador. I hugged farewell to the first round of care-givers and continued my journaling:

> My fingers are uncoordinated and I can't type worth beans. I'm stuck with a pen that jiggles and squiggles to match my erratic fingers. My left foot feels funny like it's half-connected. Makes me think I had a slight stroke in the episode I went through. Nobody told me of such, so I don't mention it. Dr. Siemens was concerned about lesions on my lungs, but no one talks of that either. My inner parts are also messed up. When Arthur urged me to go on a three-day Christian retreat where he would be speaking and I could just sit quietly, I said I hoped for a longer interlude of tranquility in our home. But I said I would be fine if he went without me.[1] *(The diary)*

This note I highlighted with stars:

> ***Arthur has shaved his beard.*** I told him he looks much younger than his 82 years without the scrub brush for which I have given him a two-year portfolio of objections. *(The diary)*

On Sunday, January 25, I hobbled on Arthur's arm through our church door in Port Ludlow, where welcome choruses rang out. Expectations were beyond rational that my fingers on the piano would play the designated keys. I was merely a lump on the bench, stumbling onto the starting notes and catching a few chords. Arthur preached a shorter-than-normal sermon and—though more than one church family invited us to lunch—got me home in record time. Back at the house in Joyce, activity was ramping up. Here's what I jotted next:

> On Monday, Janice (who'd left Dave and son Tony in Hadlock) came to attend my bedside during the daytime. She invited Marian and Elizabeth to party in the evening, which meant a Scrabble game, a jigsaw puzzle, and uproarious laughter—though I kept hearing voices telling each other to shhh. Tuesday, Dennis and Marian reported that the doctor said her baby is due any moment or might be slow-pokey like Joshua and Sarah were. Elizabeth and Bill Richardson brought their household to visit, but Liz promised to leave them all behind to spend Wednesday evening here—a break for her and company for me. Saturday, our oldest son David and his wife Vi brought their kids to visit, then all went fishing. *(The diary)*

The following Sunday, February 1, our youngest son Merton and his wife Debbie went to our church and he sang—a blessing to me even if my fingers on the piano were scarcely better than the week before. We left early from church to drive to Seattle Pacific University where Ron Guderian was being honored as the Alumnus of the Year. All the fanfare, including a reception at the president's home, left me a weary wreck. On the return drive, my husband took note of my fidgeting and said he was planning to buy a new car. "I want you to be comfortable when you are able to accompany me again in the ministry. Meanwhile..." He paused and reached across the seat to touch my hand. "I can attend the retreat without you. You can rest, just chill out, as long as you need to."

Chill out? I couldn't quite capture the concept. Times to myself have rarely occurred since I married Arthur in 1929. For within months of our marriage, God launched us on a high-speed ride of full-time ministry...while adding one child after another to our windfall of a family. In 1987, however, I could choose to settle into a *chill-out* reprieve. I could make the gift of time count. And I could leave for the children and their descendants a legacy of historical truth, abiding love, and unfettered faith.

With that perspective in my regenerating mind, I began to tread a path through my papers—half a century of epistle-length letters and scritch-scratch diaries—to revisit the lessons God has sought to teach me through His primer on faith. Perhaps even as He helped me find peace in the pressure cooker of ministry with my husband—while nurturing those entrusted to me—He would do the same for others. Thus, for kin and kind, I have untangled the threads of my experience, sorted the scraps of my learning, and stitched together a patchwork of my...well *our*...story.

I begin by looking back—way back.

Margaret Phenicie High School Graduation, 1923

PART I

LOOKING BACK—*WAY* BACK
(1925—1945)

--ONE--

Summer 1925—Tacoma, Washington

I stood facing the window, shocked to be scanning the street in anticipation. *How would I respond,* I mulled, *if Arthur came to hang out with my brother Herbert as he often did?* On this morning he was not visible and my spirits sank. I was about to turn away when there he was, scurrying up the street. At the sight of the slender, brown-haired, good-looking man clad in his tartan plaid jacket, a heart flutter stunned me.

My teenage sister Eleanor saw me hanging around Art Corey that day and was as flabbergasted as I was. She had watched me avoid him for nearly two years and had heard my snide or spiteful remarks. In fact, during that term of my antipathy Eleanor had written to our mother who was visiting relatives in Idaho:

> Arthur wanted to come over to eat and Margaret said no, he wasn't invited. He later called from the new pay phone at the gas station and I told him, "Don't waste your nickel, Margaret's not home."
>
> Love, your daughter Eleanor

My cousin Naoma, ten years older than I, stopped in while I was sticking close to Herbert and Arthur. She teased, "Is Mr. Arthur Corey not so bad after all, or did you think he might be your last chance?"

I didn't take Naoma, my 30-year-old spinster cousin, seriously. She had been my best buddy since I was the toddler she babysat, and my piano teacher from childhood on. When I was a high schooler, she pushed me to play for the small congregation of Calvary Presbyterian Church on D and South 36th St. After I graduated from Tacoma's Lincoln High School, Naoma selected a secretarial school for me and later a job in the bank. Fact is—I don't think anything happened in my early existence she was not a part of.

If those girls were dumbfounded, imagine the grin on Arthur's face when he realized my eyes were engaged in his direction. The following day I saw him with my brother, sister, and parents in the back of Calvary Church. "May I walk you home?" he asked.

Obviously, he wasn't addressing Eleanor, but she smirked, "Of course *we* would like that."

We arrived at our Phenicie residence as most of the neighborhood—my aunts, uncles and cousins—climbed down from the canvas-covered back end of Uncle Joe's 1920's Dodge truck. They had come from First Presbyterian Church where they and Art's family attended. I glimpsed their twitching eyebrows as Arthur ushered me onto my parents' porch. Before a volcano of teasing about my fiery face could erupt, I slipped into the house.

In my youth, churches were the places for revolving activities like trips to the mountains, the parks, and the harbor. So even though I played the piano and cleaned Calvary Church, I also engaged with schoolmates and cousins at First Presbyterian. This was the same cohort that had attended high school with Arthur and me. At the time of graduation, Art was sweet on the petite, popular Vera Wonderly, but she had preferred his handsome, strong, older brother Harold. It was after Harold married Vera that Arthur Corey apparently decided I showed potential as a cure for his lonely heart.

For two years, I spurned such an idea. The Coreys were from the other side of the road. Well, the other side of Pacific Avenue—the upscale side. Arthur's parents, Merton Henry and Anna Wheelock Corey, were influential in commerce, society, and politics. Merton's lineage has been traced back to Scottish ancestors in the 12th century and, in the United States, to a John Corey of New York State in 1644.

Many generations later, Merton's father was well-established as a banker in New York when, in 1888, nineteen-year-old Merton dismissed his father's job offers and moved to Tacoma. Soon after, he met Anna Phoebe Wheelock who had also travelled from Chautauqua County in New York to visit her aunt, Fanny Maria. Merton and Anna were married in 1890.

When Washington became a state, Mr. Merton Corey served two terms as a representative in the legislature. He established the first major real estate insurance business in Tacoma, and his older sons became successful in their chosen careers.

Mrs. Anna Corey's Puritan ancestors—the Wheelocks—had arrived in the New Country in the early 1600s, and the Wheelocks pioneered the establishment of academic institutions and evangelical churches in the colonies. Nearly three centuries later, in 1870, Anna Phoebe was born. Her mother, Sarah Elizabeth Vose, died in 1883, leaving thirteen-year-old Anna to look after her younger siblings.

When her own eight children were growing up, Anna Wheelock Corey became one of the founders of the Washington State PTA and was appointed its first secretary. She was President of the Lincoln PTA when Arthur and I were in school. I didn't know all that history when, a few years later, I was sneaking flirty glances at Arthur. I only knew that, in our community, the names Wheelock and Corey jumped out wherever I looked.

Mind you, my family tree has roots recorded as far back as the 1500s. My ancestors had a history of public service in the US beginning 150 years before the Revolutionary War. Some of my forebearers fought in the war for independence and some in the Civil

War. Aunt Lou Phenicie was a baby in the mid-1800s near Gettysburg when that battle broke out. She recalled hearing her parents tell of the earth-shaking, window-shattering explosions, and of an aunt's war-time project of melting down their cooking pots to make shot for the guns.

In 1889, Grandpa Charles and Grandma Julia Phenicie moved their entire household to Tacoma, transporting whatever would fit in a rickety wagon pulled by a team of horses. Prior to leaving the plains of Iowa, these grandparents had lost their farm to foreclosure and four of their children to disease or accident, three of those as young adults.[2] Grandpa's memories of his earlier years so haunted him, he said he would never go east of the Cascade Mountains, ever! Grandpa Charles kept his vow. He died three years later in 1892.

When they moved west, Herbert Samuel (Bert) was 20, Charlie Elmer, 19, and Joe, 17. Lou was 26 and married to Frank Spottswood. Their daughter Naoma was born a few years later. The family thrived in this new territory where jobs were plentiful for hard-working men. Winters were mild and summers were perfect— no comparison to the blizzards, dust storms, and heat waves of Iowa. For entertainment, the brothers fished for salmon in the harbor and in the spawning streams of the gully near their house. They were regular hikers at Mt. Rainier—at that time named Mt. Tacoma. The three brothers were rugged and robust, having survived the polio, diphtheria, and small pox that had taken their siblings and weakened their parents.

The boys reached their 30s and didn't appear to be planning on families for themselves. They occupied their time earning money and playing in the woods. Their mother, Julia, washed their clothes and cleaned up after them, while their sister Lou assisted with the cooking. Julia was not well, and Lou told them they had to take more responsibility. "I'm not going to look after you guys forever," she said, "You need to find wives."

By 1902, Bert took interest in Edith Chappell, one of the few females who participated in the Mt. Tacoma outings. On the trails, no one had to wait for Edith. Bert, impressed by her spunk, positioned himself closer to this lady than to the brothers. In 1904, when Bert was 35 and Edith 29, they were married. Naoma was their flower girl. After the wedding, the mountain treks continued. One day as the group hiked near Paradise Valley, Edith, feeling ill, remained close to the campsite. Nearby, she discovered a waterfall which no one could identify. Uncle Joe printed EDITH FALLS on a board which he nailed to a tree. The name stuck and, even yet, can be found on old Mt. Rainier maps.[3] As I calculate the dates, I realize Mother would have been expecting me and was nauseous with pregnancy!

After the first of the boys married, the idea of having a wife apparently lit a flame in the others. They, too, started pairing off with young women. The whole world on the hilltop block of 34th Street was changing. What would the Phenicies do to prepare living arrangements for all the newlyweds? Pooling resources and energy, the men constructed three houses on the large vacant parcel adjoining the original plot.

As they began their families, each of the guys selected reliable vocations. My father, Bert, became a respected member of the East Tacoma Lodge No. 89, 100F, and was employed as a baggage handler for the Union Railroad Depot. The work was hard and the hours long. In recalling those early years, I applaud his dedication while remembering his playfulness. He and I were chums.

All of the Phenicie clan were close. Good thing—since my Uncles Charlie and Joe built homes on each side of us where they raised my cousins; and my Aunt Lou, her husband and my cousin Naoma lived around the corner. According to some reports, the brothers—even before there were children—had pledged to keep relationships open and kind between all the relatives in our neighborhood, or else…whatever *or else* means.

The three homes remained until my generation moved on, and my parents' generation ended its tenure. In place of three stately structures, the Stanley & Seafort's Restaurant was established next to the iconic 34th St. bridge. At night, the restaurant sign became a beacon high above the freeway, reminding me of my uncles and aunts and cousins and parents and siblings, and of those days in the 1920s when Arthur Corey visited me, wooed me, and determined I would be Number One in his life.

Phenicie Homes, ca.1937
(125 foot logs to be used for the 34th St. Bridge, Tacoma)

--TWO--

He loves me second

A rthur elevated me to the top tier of his attention...after I had smiled in his direction. Following this sign of encouragement he occupied the spot next to my family at Calvary Presbyterian Church. His outgoing personality and tenor voice gained recognition, and music opportunities opened. My amateur piano accompaniment didn't deter the young artist—known as Mr. A.W. Corey—from wanting me on the bench when he stood to sing or lead the congregation.

On Arthur's days off, he'd ask my brother Herbert or my sister Eleanor to chaperone so we could be *alone*, whether attending the movies, hiking the hills, or picnicking at the Nisqually River. Art was so attentive, so affectionate, and so romantic! Quite the opposite of me, the girl who embraced her mother's Victorian no-public-display-of-affection attitude. When he wasn't courting me, Arthur managed a service station business on a bustling corner of Tacoma and saved his money. In anticipation of our wedding, he built a cottage at 4040 South D St., securing a loan he could pay off with his regular paychecks.

Courting Days, ca.1928

We were married at Calvary Presbyterian Church on May 25, 1929. In October—four months later—the stock market crashed, the business closed, and I was expecting a baby. Arthur—in crisis—went searching for answers, searching for peace, searching for God.

Art's inner restlessness had awakened a few years earlier during college. At the denomination-sponsored academic institution, professors derided his stance on Christ being the divine Son of God. Arthur didn't know Jesus in a personal way, but he had no doubts that the Bible was God's Word. *What a waste of intelligence, both theirs and mine,* he thought. He quit school and became a traveling salesman who demonstrated and marketed the latest fad—radios for each residence.[4] Highly motivated with desire for marriage, he simultaneously worked at other jobs, setting aside most of his earnings.

Arthur had also become disillusioned by what he perceived was the dearth of life and vitality in the First Presbyterian Church. He visited Calvary Presbyterian to hear Rev. W. F. Folsom, a recent evangelical transplant from the Free Methodist Church.

Folsom had been at Calvary a short time when he realized this congregation was merely an out-cropping of the liberal Presbyterian establishment. Most of the Calvary attendees, as well as the elders, adhered to the tenets of Holy Scripture as taught in the religious creed but had made no commitment to the Savior. "My mission," Folsom resolved, "is to speak to each person of the need to be saved."

Rev. Folsom and his message resonated for Arthur. For me, not so much.

Life had been tranquil in our little corner of Tacoma until the Great Depression of 1929 dropped the floorboards out from under everything we depended on. Arthur, having lost his income, scoured the streets for six months, searching for a job that could not be found and dying a thousand deaths with each hole the pavement wore into his single pair of shoes. A self-sufficient man from a circle of super-achievers, Arthur was humiliated by his inability to support his wife and the baby on the way, and was mortified when I returned to a part-time job cleaning Calvary Church. Frantic and fearful, he stumbled into Pastor Folsom's office. The minister quoted for Arthur the verse from Matthew 6:33: SEEK YE FIRST THE KINGDOM OF GOD AND HIS RIGHTEOUSNESS, AND ALL THESE THINGS SHALL BE ADDED UNTO YOU. The words circled round and round the track of Art's awareness as he began to observe God answering his immediate concern. First, Arthur's brother-in-law Emil Bruck secured him a job at a steel mill. Next, the Washington Cooperative Farmer Association hired him to throw sacks of feed. This was a tough assignment for a lean man, but Arthur never slowed his pace. The co-op boss was so impressed by Art's work ethic, he promoted him four times in four months until he had reached the top driver position in a department of 200 people.

In the midst of desperation and depression all around us, God was adding the things we needed. I was content in the wedding cottage—content to raise my brand-new baby, Virginia, in the security of grandparents, while basking in the social goings-on of all the aunts, uncles, and cousins. Yet Arthur continued to pursue a resolution for his seek-the-kingdom-and-righteousness question. I began to feel as if I were no longer Number One. *Why can't he relax? Where will his restlessness and urgency of spirit take him?—Take us? Will I keep up or will I lag behind, the soles of my shoes scuffing up the dust?*

God answered Arthur's quest. And, when He spoke, the dispatch came with brain-bursting clarity on a day in 1930. The account is Arthur's to tell:

> Rev. Folsom, sensing his flock needed more potent preaching, invited a Presbyterian evangelist known as the Timberland or Lumberjack Preacher. This thunder-and-lightning power supply not only urged repentance, but also invited sinners to the front—unheard of in Presbyterian circles.
>
> People were professing faith right and left, and meeting day and night for prayer and worship. I was moored in the middle of a revival. One evening in the after-service—a church back-room or home gathering of seekers—we were singing these words: *When I was lost on the mountain, barren and dark and cold, He sought the sheep that was straying. He brought me back to the fold.*[5]
>
> The presence of God was so real, I began to worship in a language I didn't know. I told God I would serve Him completely. At home I couldn't contain my enthusiasm for the Word of God and what it said to

me. My wife was furious. We had grown up in the
Presbyterian denomination. Now she thought I had
become a fanatic. *(Arthur Corey)*

Yes, Arthur *was* a fanatic. It wasn't sufficient for him to participate at Calvary alongside those of similar persuasion. My husband, with fire in his eyes, also stood up in front of his and my relatives in the circumspect and ceremonial First Presbyterian Church and told dumbfounded attendees they were paving their way to hell with all their good deeds. His dad, a Methodist, who never attended services—except at Christmas or Easter—determined to disown him. His brothers ridiculed him as irresponsible. I wanted to evaporate.

Abruptly, my hopes and expectations were falling apart. Arthur told me he knew God wanted more from him, and he was seeking to know what *more* meant. I wasn't listening. For nearly a year, I griped that Arthur preferred to be at the altar—evening after evening—rather than at home. I tried defiant tactics to dissuade him from his *irrational* all-consuming commitment. I turned a cold shoulder to his affection and muttered, "You're not the man I married."

I began listening to my parents who told me to leave my husband and bring baby Virginia to live with them. Underneath I wanted to see if my constant needling, like a dripping faucet, would cause Arthur to lose his *righteous* temper at me like he had in the church. Yet he never responded in a mean way. He was patient, kind, and loving, while I was impatient, unkind, and unloving. At last, I couldn't stand my attitude any longer and burst into tears. "Arthur," I stammered, "I have to have what you have."

Arthur read the Word and imparted his insights which I soaked up like a sponge. Both of us were buoyed by a small assembly of other resilient new converts, including his sister Hazel and her husband Emil Bruck. And we began to see God's miracles because of Art's unwavering resolve to be obedient. The first of these inexplicable, undeniable manifestations was in his own body.

This is his testimony:

Boils covered my back and a carbuncle with fistulas spread out at the base of my brain. All my life I had been sickly, plagued with sties and other skin diseases. I'd been in the hospital several times, missed school, and couldn't engage in activities with schoolmates or my brothers. Mother fed us from her garden and gave me cod liver oil. No remedy ameliorated the weakness.

After meeting God, I read passages in the Bible about healing. In April 1931, I attended the healing and evangelistic services of Charles Price at the Wooden Tabernacle in downtown Tacoma. The evangelist's declaration of the reality and relevancy of Jesus Christ to fill every need opened my understanding, and I believed my need was included in that word, *every.* I took the same message to the elders of Calvary Church and asked them to pray for me. All of them had declared faith in Christ for salvation, yet they told me miraculous healing went out with the apostles.

As I read the passages over and over and over, asking God what I was to do, it became clear that He was directing me to fast. Although I was working full-time, my intention was to go without food or drink until I was healed...or I died. On the fourth night of total fasting, when I pulled the truck into a station, the manager saw how weak I was and advised me to rest. "I will call another driver," he said.

I assured him I was to go on. The same thing happened with the manager at the next stop. But I knew God was with me.

The Lord of Heaven spoke just before I neared the Dutch Mill Café in Chehalis. The words were clear and the source unmistakable, *"Stop and eat."*

> I slammed on the brakes, then ordered a full course chicken dinner with all the trimmings. I went on my way rejoicing, with no adverse reaction in my long-empty stomach. *(Arthur Corey)*

When Arthur arrived home in the early hours, I couldn't find any sign of boils—not even scabs. I was thrilled the boils were gone, partly because I was fearful he might starve, and partly because I was comforted in the confirmation of God's words to him. The miracle added fuel to Arthur's passion for preaching. Few wanted to hear of this *Good News* which now included physical healing, and more relatives avoided or vilified him. Leaders of the denomination called him before the counsel and questioned the activities he claimed were gifts from the Holy Spirit. My husband's witness was clear and his words inspired by God. Thus the argument fizzled and their words of censure or dismissal were left unsaid.

Our second child, Marilyn, came along to divert attention when I was with our relatives, and Arthur kept busy with his night deliveries of feed and farm supplies. Long hours on the road brought opportunity for seminars from the Spirit of God. The first has been one of Art's clockwork and compelling confessions:

> Cigarettes kept me awake as I drove on isolated, dark roads. I had been smoking for years, ever since I decided inhaling and blowing was a sign of manhood. My brothers smoked, and my father was rarely without a cigar in his mouth. I knew smoking was a filthy practice and I had quit several times, throwing my packs over the bridge on 34th St. where they'd land in the depths of an inaccessible chasm. Then my eyes would search the street for a cigarette butt to smoke as I hurried to the store for a new pack. My spirit groaned within me. *How can I be dominated and contaminated by a habit so deplorable, when my heart's longing is to be fully controlled by the Holy Spirit?*

The answer came. *"Fill the void with my Word"*. Yes, Amen! I replaced the pack of cigarettes in my pocket with my New Testament. When I reached for a smoke, God's Word landed in my hand. I read under a streetlight, or with the Bible open on the steering wheel. I exercised my mouth to praise God instead of using it to pollute my lungs. The craving didn't die immediately, but I was set free. *(Arthur Corey)*

I'd never really thought much about Arthur's smoking. My dad smoked and it seemed all working men did. After Art quit, I thought, *Better to love the Bible than the cigarette that stinks up the air and costs money we don't have.* Without the stimulant of nicotine, Arthur found night driving more challenging. On one commute he fell asleep at the wheel and drove off the road and into a field near Fort Lewis. No damage resulted but—to have a clear conscience— he reported his accident to the boss, Mr. Darling. One of the top managers, seeking to fill positions with members of his religious group, said Corey was slipping and should be fired. Mr. Darling replied, "No, A.W. Corey is not slipping. You tell me, which one of your drivers would come in and report such an accident?"

After his interaction with management, Arthur was given the best day route—from Tacoma to Enumclaw, Hart's Lake, and Graham. Another driver grumbled, "I wonder how long *I'd* have to serve Jesus to have the power and influence that Corey has."

This new route took Arthur from night deliveries to tending hundreds of farmers during the day. He wasn't supposed to talk with customers about religion, but there was no regulation against talking *with* God on their behalf as he drove into their farms, nor against answering their questions. This he did with truths from the Word of God, punctuated by his testimony of healing of the infected boils, restoration of strength, and freedom from smoking.

A.W. Corey, Truck Driver, ca.1932

--THREE--

Miracles and the Marxes

Hillary and June Marx owned a farm on Arthur's route. Their story, as replayed here by Arthur, is the hallmark of the Corey ministry in the decades to come:

> One day when I delivered feed for chickens and cows to the Marx farm, Hillary wasn't home so I waited at the door for June to answer and sign the invoice. She shuffled through the door, her make-up barely disguising an appearance of death. I had known earlier she was not well. Now I learned she'd had several surgeries for cancer with no relief from the continual loss of blood. She'd been told she would never have children. "Mr. Corey," she said, "I just want to take in one more show and one more dance before I die."
>
> I was quiet a moment, then replied. "No entertainment or activity would help you. You need Jesus."

> As June clung to the door, Isaiah 53:6 came alive to
> me: HE WAS WOUNDED FOR OUR TRANSGRESSIONS, HE
> WAS BRUISED FOR OUR INIQUITIES. SURELY HE BORE OUR
> SORROWS AND BY HIS STRIPES WE ARE HEALED. I opened
> my mouth and spoke these words. "God, in Jesus
> name, heal this girl!" *(Arthur Corey)*

Arthur told me of his visit with June and that he knew God had heard. After several weeks of no apparent change in her body, June asked Art to bring the pastor, his wife, and me to visit. Together the five of us sang hymns while Hillary, a staunch Catholic, escaped to the corner. A few days later, June asked Hillary—or Hill, as she usually called him—to take her to our little church. Thinking to console his dying spouse, he left her at our evening fellowship and waited outside. After the service ended, Art asked the group to surround June for prayer, but didn't tell them the gravity of her condition.

The next time Arthur returned from the Marx's, he told me he'd discovered June dressed and scrubbing her kitchen floor. To him, she recounted her experience, "On the way home from the meeting that night, as Hill was driving near the junction towards Roy, a ball of fire came down. I could feel it flooding the area of my body with strength and health, and I burst out to Hillary, 'I think I'm dying and going to heaven.' Hill, who doesn't believe anything—not even the doctrine of his upbringing—corrected me, 'No, you are not dying. You've been healed.'"

June's health wasn't the only liberation the Marxes received. Hillary, at the time, was deeply in debt. His chickens had fowl pox and were not producing. His tractor was broken and he couldn't fix it. Slamming his tools to the ground, he fell on his knees, "God, if you are who I think you are, and if you'll show me how to put this back together, I'll turn my life over to you."

Part by part, he reassembled the tractor and it started right up. In celebration, he lit a cigarette. Then laughed as he snuffed it out, "What use is this to me?"

Hillary's home-brewed beer turned his stomach and he dumped the whole reserve. Soon after these events, Hill lost the farm to the creditors, but he had found the joy of the Lord. The couple moved into the upstairs of our home while June recuperated. In time, contrary to all medical prognosis, she gave birth to two children. Hillary Marx will have voice in another chapter, but for now I return to the timeline of our story.

Because Arthur drove during the day, he was home in the evenings with us, which, by 1934, included our third child, Elizabeth. Art also had time to be mentored by his godly pastor, Mr. Folsom, who urged him to practice preaching on the inmates at the jail and the poor at the rescue mission. Everywhere he went, Art advertised what God had wrought for the Marx couple. "What He did for June and Hillary, He can do for you."

Arthur had been driving for several years when the co-op was unionized. The union's control of businesses was absolute. Every employee and every manager had to join or would be forced to leave. The perpetrators of this ruling hounded Arthur until he had no choice. He explains:

> Because I had an exemplary record, the union organizers were initially told to leave me alone. The union boss, nicknamed River Rat, thought he could bring me around without unleashing the *goons* to work me over. Each week, after my run, he met me with the same question, "Corey, what are you gonna do?"
>
> He reminded me I had a wife and three children to provide for and I could expect a time of economic despair with so few jobs available. After three months of his harassment, I replied, "If Jesus were here, He'd be at the head of the union."
>
> "Well," River Rat retorted, "Your Jesus is different from the one I worship."

> Undeterred, I added, "Jesus' methods were love,
> joy, peace, long-suffering. What methods do you use
> to get your way? Sit down on the job? Destroy
> property? Engage in violence? Perhaps management
> is wrong in their methods, but do yours demonstrate
> the fruits of the Spirit?"
>
> River Rat barked, "A.W. Corey, you are through. Get
> out of here!"
>
> "So be it," I said, "but thank you, sir, for the last
> three months of grace." *(Arthur Corey)*

In hopes Arthur would reconsider, the company manager offered to pay his union dues, adding, "They will close us if you aren't part of the union."

Arthur had heard God's voice and his only choice was to heed that voice. I accepted my husband's resolve, sharing his belief God would provide if we sought Him first. The subsequent six months tested our faith. Art trekked far and wide looking for work until Hillary Marx procured him a job feeding chickens at the Wilcox Farm near Hart's Lake. The pay was negligible, the boarding a keeper's shack, and the children and I only saw him one day a week.

We adapted to the dismal schedule and pauper salary, but then Arthur hit me with another heart-rending arrow. God had spoken to him, calling him to become a full-time minister. The words, "FEED MY SHEEP," had come three days in a row until Arthur understood what the message meant. He'd have to quit the chicken-farm job, and we'd be totally dependent on God for our livelihood. I couldn't comprehend that God would ask this sacrifice of the father of three, with a fourth on the way. "How will we live? How will we feed the family?" I objected.

Art's confidence was so absolute he said he wouldn't make any changes until I was in harmony. I continued to protest until—in desperation for peace with God—I let go. "I don't have enough faith," I told my husband. "But I believe *you* believe. Your faith will have to be enough for both of us."

Although the Wilcox manager offered to double his pay and give him half days off for ministry, God's call reverberated in Arthur's head. He sold the house in Tacoma, gave away many of our wedding gifts and furnishings, and moved all five of us to Roy. The only place Art could find was a two-room shanty set up for employees of a logging operation. There was no water nor electricity; just a hovel with steep back steps, an outdoor toilet in the deep woods, and massive ant hills in the yard. On the positive side, at least in Arthur's thinking, was the cabin's proximity to the places we ministered—the Hart's Lake Sunday school that met in the grange hall, and a small Congregational church established earlier by the Weyerhaeuser Company.

As part of the deal with the logging boss, Art filled in temporarily for loggers who had left. He and I both knew this was not God's calling, and my husband was glum with guilt. But the manager didn't attempt to find a replacement. Machinery started to break down, and during each shift a different calamity befell the plant. After the third day of disaster, Art told the man about a Biblical character named Jonah. "Jonah was told by God to preach to sinners of Nineveh, but instead of obeying, he hid on a ship. God was displeased with Jonah and sent a storm that threatened to destroy the boat and everyone on board. The stowaway exclaimed to the captain and crew, 'I am the reason for the storm. You will have to throw me overboard so no one else is punished for my sin.'"

Arthur concluded with this warning, "Mr. Connolly, I'm like Jonah in that story. God has called me to work for Him, not for you. Even as the captain of that ship ordered his crew to dump Jonah, you must let me go, or you too will be tormented."

When my husband came through our door, his face glowed and his words resonated. "Was that man ever glad to get rid of me. And am I ever uplifted in the freedom to seek *first* the kingdom of God, and *only* the kingdom of God!"

Soon after, Arthur received a tentative offer from Seattle to sing over the air in a daily program and to lead the songs during meetings held at night. The opportunity to use his dynamic tenor voice in ministry sounded sensible, as did the idea of a regular salary. But Art knew the region of Eatonville and Roy and McKenna and Kapowsin—small former logging communities located southeast of Tacoma—was where we belonged. We would remain among locals who looked to him as an authority—as one who lived what he preached.

Weyerhaeuser Congregational Church, Eatonville, ca.1935

Speaking of authority and living it…we sometimes drove by the McKenna Charleston Inn which we'd heard was a veritable den of iniquity. One day Arthur saw inebriated young people hanging on each other as they streamed from the doors and into the parking lot. He parked the car, fell to his knees, and urged God to close its doors. His exact words were, "God, in the Name of Jesus Christ, smash this thing all to hell!"

God replied. The next week, the Christian owner of the gas station across the street told us the police had locked the doors. Arthur added his interpretation for our assembly on Sunday. "What a proof that God hears our prayers of faith and exercises His power over the forces of evil."

When we told Arthur's mother what had transpired, we watched a smile spread across her face. "You know," she said. "Your great-grandfather on the Wheelock side was a circuit-rider reverend who closed many doors of booze halls and saloons in the Texas Territory."

Art learned that the owner of the Charleston Inn was looking for someone to move in and keep the hall free of vandalism, and that he'd charge no rental fees. We relocated from the shack to the Inn, sleeping in the guest rooms, and turning the dance hall with its green bar stools into a meeting place. There was space for the people and preaching, room for the piano and singing. The three girls, at seven, five, and three years old, jumped into the ministry, using their voices and learning to sing in harmony. "Please," they begged, "can we also go with Daddy to sing at the rescue mission?"

I helped them memorize all five verses of a hymn and they got their wish.

The outreach in the area grew and new believers, including Hillary Marx, took responsibility. God also sent the Neufeldts, a young couple from Alberta, Canada, who were looking for a ministry to lead. Arthur, sensing it was time to move on, continued to seek direction. One morning, God sent a clear message: *"Go see Dr. Roy Brumbaugh."*

Art had not yet met Dr. Brumbaugh but had taken notice of his reputation, for this clergyman had also ignited the ire of the elders at First Presbyterian Church. A highly educated minister, Brumbaugh had been recruited from the East Coast to First Presbyterian, one of the largest denominational churches on the West Coast. His message of repentance and salvation immediately threw the staid and stiff rule makers of the denomination into a tailspin. When their dictates threatened to squeeze Brumbaugh dry, he announced his resignation. Abandoning all the benefits of his position, the unconventional cleric led nearly half of the congregation, more than 700 people, across the alley from First Presbyterian Church into the Scottish Rite Temple. They named their group the Independent Bible Church of Tacoma. Many of the First Presbyterian elders and leaders and teachers, and all of the new believers participated in the move that one compatriot titled "An Exodus."

The mandate to find Brumbaugh burned in Arthur's brain until he found the pastor—not in the church during office hours, but at home. Here's his report:

> When Dr. Brumbaugh's wife told him I'd come because I had been sent by God, the pastor flew down the stairs three steps at a time. He gave full attention as I explained how God had booted me out of the same church years earlier; how He had proven His call through miracles; and how He'd put in my heart a desire to serve as a missionary in an unchurched area. Brumbaugh told me, "I have mission leaders in my congregation who are looking for a minister with precisely that calling."
>
> I soon met the three financial businessmen. "Praise the Lord," they said. "We were asking God to lead us to a devoted follower of Christ who is committed to reaching the lost in our homeland. We will support you with goods, finances, whatever..."
>
> That was my touch point to interrupt them, "I'm not concerned about finances. God will provide for us. Just tell me where the need is greatest. I'm ready to go."
>
> "We will pray and God will enlighten," one replied. "But first, I wonder if you could give your testimony to the women of the congregation. Many of them are suffering from the shredding of their families over the church split. God's faithfulness to you may be the message they need to hear." *(Arthur Corey)*

Arthur was surprised by the request. He'd never formally spoken to an audience larger than a room full of derelicts at the mission, but he agreed. When he came home from the ladies' gathering, he replayed the event:

> I had a message in hand and a sense of the Lord's presence when I looked over that audience of 300 women whose faces mirrored the sorrow in their spirits. I opened my mouth to speak, but instead my voice choked with emotion and I began to weep. I reached for a handkerchief as tears gushed. Frozen in place, I was totally confounded at my inability to gain control. Then the women started to cry, first a few, then a throng. I stepped down from the pulpit and stood with them, watching God mend their broken hearts. After most of the women had left, Mrs. Brumbaugh spoke, "This is what we needed. God used your tears to loosen ours." *(Arthur Corey)*

As he relayed the events for me, Arthur's eyes filled and so did mine. He continued, "I was still so broken up, I couldn't even answer Mrs. Brumbaugh. I could only nod."

I wiped my eyes as he concluded, "I'd been humbled to that of a weeping—not preaching—prophet."

Arthur began to meet regularly with Pastor Brumbaugh[6] and his elders, finding a kindred spirit of consecration. One day, Art received a special invitation from the mission committee. They told him a Mr. Nichols of the Independent Bible Church (IBC) of Port Angeles had contacted them, and would Arthur consider assisting while Pastor Ben Hutchinson was on sabbatical.

Arthur began a regular commute to the Olympic Peninsula from our location in the converted Charleston Inn, allowing me to remain near Tacoma until after the birth of our fourth child. Thus it was that three churches played part in the foundation of Arthur's faith: First Presbyterian, where his family and some of my relatives attended, Calvary Presbyterian, where Arthur committed himself to the Lord, and Independent Bible of Tacoma, where he received the call to move to the Olympic Peninsula.

When David was a few weeks old, Arthur settled all of us into the parsonage in Port Angeles. We assisted at IBC, held meetings at the jail, and commenced Bible studies in the country. Within the year we moved to Joyce, the place God had prepared for us to establish roots, raise our family, and work for Him. We sought His kingdom always, and waited…sometimes longer than we liked…for Him to provide all things, whether food for the table—which I will write about later—or provisions for the outreach, the subject of the next chapter.

Grange House Sunday School, 1939.
Family members include:
Back row: center—Virginia Norman with David Corey; right—Margaret Corey
Center row: dark, bobbed hair—Marilyn Corey
Front row: standing—Elizabeth Corey; far right—Virginia Corey

--FOUR--

Provisions for the journey

A fter June Marx was healed of cancer—as reported earlier—and her husband Hillary pledged his heart to the Lord, they became ministers. Their effective leadership freed Arthur from ministry responsibilities near Roy. We'd been settled at Joyce for seven years when Hillary asked Arthur to consider a missionary expedition across the United States as far as Kentucky where they had mutual friends. Arthur agreed to seek the guidance of God. The year was 1945; the country was at war and the neighborhood uneasy; and we were prosperous in children—eight of them—but impoverished in purse.

Art felt assurance the timing was right. God would care for the widow and fatherless left behind, and would supply whatever the two men lacked for the journey.

Arthur has often reiterated the missionary-journey story of 1945, and with each telling, he has recalled additional encounters experienced during his six-week trip with Mr. Marx. Thus, to ensure a comprehensive accounting of God's profound direction, interaction, and enabling, I have ceded to my husband—the one

blessed with Scrabble-word skill to match his meticulous memory—
the entirety of this chapter:

Hillary (Hill) Marx asked me to mentor him on a journey, traveling in the apostles' way. We would have one change of clothes and no money for sustenance. We would accept rides as God provided. We would not lift a hitchhiking thumb.

I left home on foot in a heavy wool suit and no alternate outfit. I jangled a few coins in my pocket, knowing the total of 82 cents would be enough for the ferry crossing. "Father," I asked, "prior to my arrival at Hillary's, would you provide a set of clothes cool enough for the heat and humidity of a Midwest summer?"

The first ride took me to Port Angeles where I met an old acquaintance on the street. He invited me into his office where we prayed together for his wayward daughters. As I left, he handed me $10. The second ride took me to Sequim where I saw the Langendorf bread truck. I expected the driver to be Forrest Aldrich; instead it was his son. Willard offered me a front-seat ride, and for the next hour he re-lived and re-enacted the horrors and trauma of war in the South Pacific from which he had recently been released. Tears flowing, he told how God had spared him when hundreds were dying all around. "I've done nothing worthwhile since," he lamented. "I feel like I am a total failure in God's eyes."

As Willard drove, I placed my hand on his shoulder, "Dear Father, Thou art the healer and the source of joy—true joy. Please mend your child's heart and bring him peace."

When we got to Four Corners, Willard offered to take me farther. "No need," I said. "I'll catch another ride to the ferry."

He gave me $18.00 and snuffled, "If my dad were here, he would give you more."

As I started away, he pulled out another $10. Altogether it was the exact amount for a summer suit costing $34.00, and a straw-woven hat at $4.00. Clad in garments I'd asked God to supply, I joined Hillary Marx and we were on our way east.

We bumped around in the back of an empty box truck as far as Renton, south of Lake Washington. When we crawled out, both Hill and I reached out to shake the hands of the driver and his associate, and to give each of them gospel pamphlets—we carried a few hundred—as well as New Testaments. At the same moment the two fellows pushed similar handouts toward us. The driver laughed, "This is a first in all our years of seeking to share the Good News with travelers—hitchhikers seeking to evangelize us!"

Our first days of travel we went from town to town, sharing our message of hope in Jesus with drivers and everyone else we met. We prayed for those who asked. We received donations *without* asking, usually adequate to get us to the next God-directed stop.

After a week in fellowship with each other and those we met, we arrived in Wyoming—to uninhabited deserts, barren cattle ranges, never-ending dirt roads, and the first inhospitable driver. The motorist, a leathery grim-faced rancher, ushered us into the back of his pickup. When we came close to the pre-determined crossroads, the pick-up went into high gear and roared on through. "Stop," I yelled over the ruckus of flying gravel.

The driver ignored me, and I turned to Hill. "Do you suppose he's high-jacking us as workers?"

The rancher had already told us he was short of help and planned to collect a hired hand who'd been on a drunken binge. Nodding to Hill, I slipped over the driver's side, stepped onto the running board, reached in the window, and snatched the ignition key. With that, the truck lurched to a halt. Not wanting to create additional fuel for dispute, we thanked the stunned hostage taker for the ride and started back toward the crossroad.

We trudged the rest of the day until we arrived at a tiny town with one small hotel. Discovering there was no room, we sat on the front porch chairs. The manager said, "You plan to stay here?"

"We see no other option."

"Maybe you can sleep in the new jail not yet in use," he said.

The caretaker opened the door to a cell. Not at all comfy—merely a blanket on strips of woven steel. Counting the seconds during wretched, wakeful hours I thought of Paul who had been sick and bound in prison at the instigation of rabble rousers. My conclusion: our discomfort in the jail was God's provision and our choice—not that of an angry mob. I could give no protest.

At 3:30 AM, I awakened Hill to get going. We tramped and tramped and tramped. No one stopped. Then a cloud of billions of freshly-hatched mosquitoes engulfed us, forcing us to run and swat, run and swat, until too fatigued to fight off the monsters.

In the distance, we noticed a trail on the hillside where a sheep herder stood next to a canvas-covered pioneer-style wagon. A finger of smoke drifted upward. We trudged in the direction until we heard the shepherd yell, "Breakfast will be ready when you get here."

A feast. Hot cakes, bacon, and eggs—right by the camp stove. The man was dying for company and we were dying of hunger. "How can you do this in rationing times?" I asked.

"Not to worry. Please eat."

"Do you mind if I pray? I'd choke if I didn't thank the Lord," I said.

I asked God's blessing on the food and on the kind man who was willing to apportion it. Refreshed, Hillary and I went on our way. We hiked the sunbaked road mile after mile. Automobiles and pickups and transport trucks whizzed by—all those drivers paying no attention to two plodding travelers. Out of his own despair and an ugly mood, Hill blurted, "What was that promise of protection God gave you?"

I didn't answer him immediately. Too tired, too spent to comment, too done-in to voice a request to heaven. Guilt hit me in the gut. *Where was my faith? How had I forgotten*? Humbled, I looked upward. "Yes, Lord, you did promise: THE SUN SHALL NOT SMITE YOU BY DAY. Thank you for honoring your Word."

Within minutes, a cloud formed over us and drizzled rain. No rain elsewhere, only where we walked or curled up in the ditch for a siesta. Hill cheered, "Now, wouldn't it be a miracle if someone came down from the mountain and took us back into the hills."

Out of those heights a rig thundered towards us and stopped. "You fellas need a ride? My stop is half hour ahead and I'll return for you."

The driver took us into the foothills, listening and nodding as we told how God had brought us to this place. I declared, "God will bless you because of your kindness to these wayfaring preachers."

He left us at a tavern near the crossroads. "Thank you for the pleasant company. I wish you well."

We entered and sat at the bar, hoping to get a sandwich. No server was available, leaving us to speculate what God had in store for this stop. We needn't have questioned divine guidance. Nearly an hour later, a frazzled lady came from the back. She said, "My husband has been taken to the hospital, and I don't know how to run this place. I was hoping you would leave."

I introduced us as ministers of the gospel. "We know that God loves us, all of us, and He hears and answers our prayers."

God had prepared her heart and we saw her turn to the Lord in faith for salvation and in courage to believe for her husband. After lunch, her son came and took us to a hotel in Laramie where we paid $1.00 each for a good night's sleep.

The next day the Spirit said, *"Go into the café for a meal—a real meal."*

Our pockets were empty but I didn't question that well-known voice. At the counter a railroad engineer sat down beside me. I offered him a Christian pamphlet which he took a few minutes to read. He looked up, "What church you represent, boys?"

I said, "One God, One Jesus, One Spirit."

"Yes, mm, yes, yes. That's right." He paused. "You goin' over the mountains? Be at the railroad in 30 minutes."

He covered the fare for our *real meal,* and we headed for the station. Clueless about the cargo train, we crawled into a coal car. Minutes from the station we were inundated in coal dust and choking to breathe. When the locomotive stopped at a water station to refill the steam engine, we found a lumber car and rode through the highlands under the shelter of gigantic beams. At the next station, as we waited for the steam to start and the clankety-clank to begin, two workers saw us stowaways hunkered under the wood. One, instead of confronting us or informing us that we'd be going nowhere, motioned toward another train headed for Denver.

In Colorado Springs we met a pastor who invited me to preach at his church. Afterward, a lady from the congregation insisted we visit a radio evangelist in Missouri—two states away. But first, we walked for hours between half-hour rides until we arrived at the next state, Kansas. The excitement of the people we met in Wichita was palpable. From them we ascertained the war with Japan had ended, and our spirits also were uplifted. I wondered how my dear ones were celebrating, and felt stitches of homesickness to enhance the hunger in my gut. For we had not eaten in two days and one night.

We came upon a dairy stand and spent our meager coins for a quart of milk. A little farther down the road we saw a sign for watermelons. Perhaps there would be damaged or unmarketable produce. At the truck farm, a lady in a long, garden-stained dress looked at two skinny, sweaty, dusty wanderers and asked, "How long since you've eaten?"

"Thirty-nine hours to be exact," I replied.

"Give me half hour and I'll have food for ya."

We crashed under a tree until we heard, "Well, come in and get it or I'll throw it out the window!"

We were washed up and eating when she asked, "You guys are preachers, aren't you?"

Next we knew, she had gathered the adults of her family to hear us share the gospel. I don't know the results of the meeting, but God does. I only know we were on the way to Springfield, Missouri, energized by full bellies. Of course, they were empty again by the time we arrived at the residence of the radio evangelist in Springfield. Even as the lady in Colorado had indicated, the preacher had been prepared by God to receive us. We stayed there four days, assisted in his radio program, and participated in his services. I'm not sure his wife had been equally prepared by God, as she appeared inconvenienced by the extra cooking and intense conversation...at least at the beginning. Once she received a blessing, she turned our stay into a place of retreat before we headed further east.

On the way to Kentucky I asked the Lord if he would supply the funds needed for the toll bridges at the southern tip of Illinois. He didn't give us the money. Instead He timed the lifting of the toll just prior to our arrival. I don't suppose the officials knew they were God's instruments on our behalf.

When we arrived at the next town we asked an unkempt lady on the street about possible accommodations. She pointed us to a tent meeting about to begin, and said, "Those people will help you."

Crowds were gathered outside the tent, among them many star-struck followers pushing themselves towards the popular evangelist. We introduced ourselves and the kingpin issued an invitation to share the platform. Turns out all the *saved* people were on stage. The rest, unsaved or backslidden, including the evangelist's wife, were relegated to the lower level. They needed—as per the doctrine of this group—to be saved for the first time, or saved again from their backslidden condition. Singing was accompanied by wild dancing, and the music leader seemed to direct one of the songs in our direction: "Get the devil outta here, get the devil outta here…."

Her words sloshed off our unfazed ears like water. Testimonies began around the platform. We gathered that the most demonstrative speakers were considered the most spiritual. Only one stooped, frail man sounded truly genuine, but his subdued testimony set off a domino train of yawns. We, however, were ignored. At 10:00 PM the evangelist launched into his sermon reiterating several times how God had brought him to this town. He preached and he paced and he waved his arms…on and on. Suddenly, he stopped mid-sentence. "Folks," he said, "I'm out of order. We have two visiting brethren. They are of God. I'm turning the meeting over to them."

Hill and I reported the encounters of our trip, and God moved in the meeting. The evangelist's wife confessed her sin, and the singing lady chanted, "It's of the Lord, of the Lord, of the Lord…"

By 1:30 AM most of the people had left, but not the humble, bent-over man. "You need a place to stay? Come with me!"

He led us by flashlight through a cornfield maze to a humble shack and gave us straw ticks on a wooden platform. Our eyes had barely closed when I awakened to his voice. "Time to get up boys, breakfast is on."

It was 4:00 AM, and his wife had set a table. After I asked God's blessing on the meal and this couple, the man teared up, "This is the way it ought to be, the way it ought to be."

We traversed through whiskey territory, encountering drunks, ruffians, and outlaws, to whom we gave the Word...or space...as God directed. Our trail ended in Oakdale, Kentucky, at a Free Methodist school—the only pre-determined stop on our mission. There we visited the Whitehouse sisters who, as teachers, were on summer break. Ten years earlier they had assisted us in the little Weyerhaeuser chapel near McKenna, Washington. Hill and I expended four days of energy and know-how to maintenance on campus, while eating regularly scheduled meals and sleeping comfortably each night.

Hillary's wife sent word to the school that their child was ill and Hill was needed. We reversed our direction. On the road west our first cabbie, a shoe salesman, opened his mouth to preach as soon as we closed the door. When we tried to tell him of our missionary journey, he said we were putting on an act. "Ha," he said, "you look like hooligans, not holy men."

His sermon continued while we listened and smiled and tossed in a Scripture when he paused to catch a breath. The evangelizing peddler must have changed his opinion, for as he dropped us off he tucked a five-dollar bill into my hand.

Hill and I spent a night in the YMCA and separated the next morning, thinking drivers might more readily stop for one straggler than two, and two routes to Denver would double the opportunity to minister. My first offer of a ride came from a wicked man whose mouth spewed the vilest language I'd ever heard...all the way to Kansas. I sang hymns to drown out his offensive words the rest of that day and into the night—more than 750 miles. He finally let me escape near a gas station that had closed for the night. Close by, I encountered a family headed for Denver. Using my flashlight, I waved down the next car to pass on the highway. When I explained the family's need for fuel, the driver said he lived nearby and his neighbor would have gas. I asked, "May I ride over with you?"

I handed the Good Samaritan cash to pay for the five gallons we took from his neighbor. After one more service stop, I disembarked in Denver at the office of Hillary's associate.

Hill arrived presently and told his tale. "I waited eight hours for my first ride," he said. "Once I was seated, I could see the one-armed driver was stupefied with drink. He slurred and stuttered that he'd come from Nova Scotia in Canada and was in a hurry to get to San Francisco to find his brother. He was in a hurry all right, and drove like a maniac—way beyond the speed limit and all over the road, his one hand clutching a whiskey bottle and the wheel. I was petrified."

Hill's face revealed the anguish of his ride and I affirmed my understanding. He continued, "When the guy stopped in the middle of nowhere for a hitchhiking sailor, I went to the back seat and continued calling out to God in my spirit. A flat tire brought the car to a halt, whereupon the driver got into an argument with the sailor, who stomped off. I climbed back in the front seat next to the sobering sot. He listened to my testimony and gave his heart to the Lord. I taught him Scripture the rest of the way."

Hillary and I split up again in Denver, heading in two routes toward home. I was picked up by a burly rancher who seemed interested in hearing of my ventures. At noon we stopped for dinner and he told me, "Price don't mean nothin'. Get what you want."

I thanked him and thanked God for the meal. Then Joe told me his story. He had been a ranch foreman, responsible for a large group of black employees. One of the white girls in town said she had been raped by a black man. She couldn't identify the perpetrator, so the mob took one of Joe's workers and dragged him through the town until he died. Since that day, Joe had been tormented by nightmares and remorse. "Why didn't I stop them? Why didn't I rescue him?" he repeated over and over.

I looked into his eyes and opened my hands. "No sin or failure is too hard for God to forgive."

He nodded. "My wife is a Christian. She's been praying a long time."

The redeemed rancher and I sang hymns at the top of our lungs all the way down the Rocky Mountains. And the angels echoed our chorus.

I continued to sing in eagerness as I returned home to my family. For them, the six weeks had seemed interminably long and the shortage of food burdensome. But as God had promised, His grace was sufficient. He had led Hillary and me, and He had provided enough for the well-being of the priceless heritage I had left behind. *(Arthur Corey)*

PART II

OUR HERITAGE
(1930s-1970s)

--FIVE--

A parade of daughters and sons

Eight years prior to Arthur's trip with Mr. Marx, my husband and I moved from Tacoma to Port Angeles with our first four children: Virginia, Marilyn, Elizabeth, and David. Within a few months, our ministries were growing in the outlying communities of Eden Valley and Joyce, and our year of commitment to the Independent Bible Church would soon expire. Arthur learned that the abandoned Ramapo Grange Hall on a quarter-acre lot was up for auction at the Clallam County Court House. To him the property—located midpoint between Eden Valley and Joyce—had the potential to function as an abode for his family, a sanctuary for services, and a roadside haven for neighbors. I wasn't convinced—the place was in shambles—but I could give no argument when Arthur was certain of God's guidance. My vow to him still held. I would trust my husband's faith to be ample enough to fill the gaps in mine.

At the auction, a bystander told Arthur he should bid what he had in hand—$28. No other contenders emerged to cover the full $100 of back taxes, so Arthur cleaned his pocket in exchange for the ownership papers.

It was one thing to become owner of a junk yard and another to make it livable as a home. So after the purchase came the purging. Arthur and a pal named Art Berg shoveled and burned mounds of garbage—the remnants of the facility's eons-earlier existence as a meeting place for farmers, a temporary classroom for high schoolers…and a luxury suite for rats, bats, and spiders.

When we moved into the grange house, it was complete with stoves and windows and cupboards, but no running water, no plumbing, no electricity. Rain siphoned through a splintered roof of the second floor we used as a bedroom, and wind whistled through the shriveled walls on every side. The first winter we froze, and the following summer we suffocated. Nonetheless, we chose to give thanks for the favorable and fix what we could of the faulty. This former grange became our meeting hall, and folks came from around the community and as far away as Port Angeles to our Sunday school class. (We couldn't call this structure a church for lack of legal certification.)

We'd been settled for a few months when a delegation from Calvary Presbyterian Church in Tacoma visited. Ten camped out for two nights in our over-sized living room. These friends wanted to see how we were settled and to hear Arthur tell of the local ministry. Of course, my husband obliged.

One guest asked, "A.W., how are you supporting your family?"

"God is providing *all* of our needs," Arthur said, "and I know HE WILL COMPLETE THAT WHICH HE HAS BEGUN."

I squelched my thought, *'Tis fortunate we have the supply of canned beans from Hazel's garden to accompany the food the guests brought.* Because by this time, food was becoming for us a limited commodity.

Thus began a decade when my faith would be profoundly tested. There were winters during those early years we ate canned beets twice a day, or oatmeal thrice a day, or green beans for a week—at least that's what my offspring argue…or exaggerate. I, however, will never forget the supper hour that Arthur had us sing *Praise God from whom all blessings flow* over the empty flour bin.

Nor will I forget the mealtime Art asked me to bless the food—which amounted to a widow's morsel. All I could say to God was, "*Will* you give us our daily bread?"

Likewise, I won't forget how God replied. After we sang the doxology, we discovered bread-filled bags on our doorstep. After I specifically asked God for our daily bread, he awakened a young woman and sent her as an emissary with a supply of bread and flour and sugar and coffee—the latter not even on my ask-the-Lord list.

When I think how God now meets our needs and even our wants, my addled attic aspires to put to rest the hardships of life from the late 30s into the 50s—those years of depression and war and scarcity of sustenance, those years before we had a garden and animals and the ingenuity to surmount the obstacles to managing a farm. As one neighbor of those days said to another, "Those Coreys may have some skills, but none I can see when it comes to farming."

No, we were not initially gifted in growing gardens—we learned by trial and irritating error.

We were, conversely, proficient in producing babies. In 1940, our son John was born, taking from David the position as caboose—a nomenclature recommended by one of the teachers. Secretly I had concurred, and wrote to my cousin Naoma:

> Maybe John is the tail end or caboose, as I had thought David might be. Not that we don't love our children, it's just that the world is in such turmoil. Every day we hear of invasions and wars initiated by men with evil hearts. The future for our children and our country is so uncertain... Love, Marg

International tensions exacerbated local uneasiness and intensified my own distress. In December 1941, when the US went to war, I was showing signs of another pregnancy. Phillip joined the family in 1942 during this era of global warfare and Corey deprivation. When he was a few months old, well-off friends— thinking to ease our food deficit and wishing for a boy of their own—offered to adopt him. In the generation before me the concept of children from large, poor families being adopted by the rich was not unusual. I was stunned, nevertheless, both by the request and by the recognition that I was into yet another pregnancy. In 1943, Phillip was only 15 months when I gave birth to our seventh, Eleanor Joy. Her arrival prompted my father-in-law to reprove Arthur for lack of self-control. Arthur swallowed the retort that entered his mind, *Well Dad, you had eight, of which I am your seventh.* Instead he spoke these words, "Remember the Lord said to populate the earth."

His dad was equally astute, "Well, God didn't expect you to do the whole job."

Before two more years had passed, Merton was born. In five years of wartime worry, 1940—1945, I'd welcomed—albeit with consternation and ignominy—four children to trail the older four. It was then that I chose to turn away from the contempt of neighbors whose entire families numbered three or four and I determined to quit apologizing to my cousin, my sister, and my mother. Within months of Merton's birth, God answered my most urgent entreaties. The war ended upon the surrender of Germany and Japan, and Arthur returned from the expedition already portrayed. We became the owners of 21½ acres of property, sliced through by two streams of fresh water, canopied with timber, and sporting enough wood to keep stove fires burning forever. The children would no longer have to haul water from a neighbor's creek or search for firewood of bark and log splinters along the railroad grade after the logging trains passed by. As God gave opportunity and offerings over the next months, we bought a cow and planted a garden.

Family Photo, 1945
Back: Virginia, Elizabeth, Merton, Marilyn
Front: John, Eleanor, Phillip, David, 1945

In the spring of 1946, Arthur, the man of vision and a thousand ideas, remarked, "We can take apart the house we live in and use the materials to build a place on the property."

I knew better than to sound argumentative. I simply questioned, "How is that possible? We have no truck, no jalopy, no donkey to transport the boards. We'll end up with no place to live when the rains come."

The discussion proceeded long into the night, but my husband's resolve was set and he gave the last word...or should I say paragraph. "We'll build in the style of a barn to be used for animals and hay after God supplies the wherewithal to build a real house. I've measured the length of boards and two-by-fours we can take off to get started. We'll have plenty of room to live here during the construction."

Last Days at Grange House, 1946
John, Mert, Phil, Eleanor, David

After that declaration, he set the process in motion. Marilyn (14), Elizabeth (12), and David (9) collected corner stones from the creek and felled and peeled trees for foundation logs, while Arthur went to meet Virginia (16) on her way home from Prairie High School in Alberta, Canada. Upon their arrival, the entire clan got in on the arduous assignment of tearing apart roofing, pulling off boards, and straightening nails…followed by the abysmal task of lugging each piece a quarter mile down the county road in plain view of the entire highway population.

As I had anticipated, rains fell, floods rose, and blizzards blew long before the place was sealed. Actually, it never was fully sealed, yet we lived in this barn-style farmhouse for the next 12 years. The animals couldn't wait for the farmhouse to be repurposed on their behalf, so we put together a pole and shake barn not far from the farmhouse—both of which stand today as a testament to my husband's and my sons' architectural learn-as-you-go aptitude.

During the dozen years in the farmhouse, though it never repelled the weather, we engineered upgrades. We plumbed the house with running water which we heated in pipes passed through the firebox of the cast iron cook stove. We installed a bathtub behind a curtain and put away the round galvanized bathtub in

The Farmhouse of 1946-1958
Marian

which we'd bathed—one after another—for years. The Public Utilities District (PUD) connected electricity, and the Pennoyers donated a refrigerator, radio, and toaster. They also delivered an antique fold-into-cupboard bed which we returned to their relatives who expressed sentimental attachment. The only common necessity we never achieved was an indoor toilet.

In 1947, Marian was born, and five years later—after I was beyond age—I gave birth to our tenth, Janice. The summer of 1952, soon after Janice arrived, Arthur cogitated on the construction of a *real* house on our acreage. I was so overwhelmed by the demands of a baby and all the other youngsters, I muttered under my breath, *that man's imagination has over-taken his intellect.* When he persisted, I spoke, "New materials would cost thousands—tens of thousands!"

I pointed to the numbers on the chalkboard by the stove. "We can't even pay down the debt to the co-op for the few farm supplies we must have."

"God will make a way," Arthur answered. "The vision is becoming clear and I'm asking for your trust."

I began to fill page after page in my diary with the enterprise of new construction. We blasted enormous stumps out of the ground; smoothed a south-exposure location where the sun would shine in the windows; and purchased and rebuilt a long-defunct sawmill to cut our own lumber. Our children worked alongside their dad while other family and friends added physical labor, used and new materials, and donations. I recorded the zigzag of advancement—two steps forward and as many backward—until six long years later, in the summer of 1958, we moved our appliances and furniture into the shell of a structure. The Big House was far from finished, but finally we had an indoor toilet...two of them in fact! No longer would I—with red-faced chagrin—send guests along the path to a malodorous outhouse.

My memory cache overflows with recollections of loving, disciplining, and surviving a ménage of ten children who shared our curious living conditions of the 30s to the 50s. They grew up with limited resources, yet became masters of invention. They repurposed broken-down equipment; invented new ways of doing old tasks; and turned throwaway clothes into fashionable wardrobes. They learned to cook, to construct, and to lead. Recognizing my inadequacy to organize those tales, I hereby entrust to the scrolls of another scribe[7] most of the escapades, challenges, and victories of those ten, marshalling for these pages merely a morsel.

Nonetheless, I must express my gratitude to God for all the fulfilled assurances He gave to Arthur and me, the most glorious of which is knowing that each of our children loves the Lord.

'Twas not always so.

--SIX--

All your children are in

The path of our offspring to Jesus took ten trails. Each person could point to a milepost of direction—perhaps at an earliest imprinted memory, or perhaps later when recognizing their parents' faith wouldn't save them. I have chosen to include, as an example, the journey of one of them, Merton Henry. For it was he, our eighth child and youngest son, that kept Arthur and me humbly asking God to reach his heart.

To retrace the pathway of Merton I reflect back in time to his beginnings in 1945. And from there I track a twenty-year passage that could be painted as a winding trail of potholes, quicksand, and detours—not unlike the traveler's journey in John Bunyan's *The Pilgrim's Progress*—until God won the victory.

From toddlerhood on, Merton balked when told what to do, rebelled at being corrected, and only pretended to listen when God's Word was spoken. He roughhoused his sister Marian until she cried—though she was equally to blame for pestering him. He

Merton, Janice, and Marian, ca.1956

instigated trouble in school, frustrated his teachers, and lost his cool during sports.

But my son Mert approached with equal ingenuity and gusto all projects—whether in work or in play—as noted in the first example:

On Thanksgiving weekend, 1960, Mert (15) and Phil (18) took the small Ford tractor across the wooden bridge over our rain-enriched swollen creek. Leftovers from an earlier era of tree-felling had caught their attention. Too rotten for home fires, the logs could be used to fortify the dam in the creek a few feet downstream from the bridge…or so the boys reasoned. They began to tug logs behind the tractor onto the bridge, then roll them over the side, creating a whale-breaching splash ten feet below. An hour into this hard work of entertainment Phil quit, while Mert said, "I'll just move a few more."

Phil had barely warmed up by the stove when he jerked to attention. Anxiety overcame him and he flew out the door. From the porch he heard a soft, distant voice calling, "Help! Help!"

"Dad!" Phil yelled. "Mert is hurt! At the creek!"

Arthur and Phil jumped in the car. They sped across the yard, slammed the brakes at the top of the hill by the original farmhouse, and rushed toward the creek—no longer hearing the call for help. Our oldest son, David, and I ran after them. All the way I cried out to Jesus for His mercy.

When Phil reached the bottom of the hill, his heart pounded with anticipation of the worst. He could see one of the bridge's two support logs had broken in half and the decking hung sideways toward the creek. The wheels and underside of the tractor faced upward, way below what was left of the bridge. A dam of water was backing up behind the timbers that were pinned under the weight of the tractor. Then he caught a glimpse of Mert's face in the frigid, rising water. A cedar railing log had jammed his arm between the front and back wheels and his entire body was submerged. But his eyes were moving!

Phil slid down the bank and yanked at the end of the log, fearing it would be lodged too tightly to be moved, and he'd not be able to save his brother. To his amazement, the beam easily released Mert's arm. The wood and the tractor had been laid perfectly to protect the boy from being crushed. David and I arrived as Phil and Art tugged our shivering, white-faced teen out of the water and onto the bank. What a manifestation of God's protection, and what a deliverance! The tractor needed considerable fixing, but not the boy. *Thank you, Jesus.*

A quarter of a century later, I can still visualize the smashed bridge, twisted tractor, and uninjured youth. I know God orchestrated each measure of his rescue.

Did our son hear God speak as the water rose over his face? If so, it was not apparent when his buttons of provocation were pushed by others—in particular Ricky, our foster child.

In 1959—the year before Merton's tractor accident—Ricky, the first of three boys had arrived. The welfare had asked us to take the six-year old, whose behavior could not be controlled by his disabled mother. As a family, we had opened our hearts, treated Ricky as our own, and tried to help him overcome his proclivity for theft and lies. Merton, however, tended to deal with Ricky's hyperboles through mockery. That big-brother style continued long past Merton's water rescue and into 1962 when Edward and Stacey Raub arrived.

Several years earlier, these two young sons of a large Native American family had been removed from their family by government decree. By the time we were asked to take them, they'd already been battered, beaten, and bruised by abusive guardians. They needed a stable environment, and we stumbled along in efforts to provide a haven, while keeping them occupied on the farm and out of mischief.

When it was necessary for me to leave the boys under Merton's supervision, I worried over what reports would await me. *Would I hear of misdeeds of the boys? Or of Merton stretching the boundaries of conventional discipline?* Those days, when I returned after leaving the boys under my son's jurisdiction, my typical notation in the diary was: I'm GLAD to be home and ALL is intact.

In 1963, Merton graduated from Crescent High School in Joyce. His grades earned him valedictorian honors that required a speech. Rather than prepare a talk, he occupied his time by testing out a new tractor, working at Crescent Beach Resort, clearing land behind Joyce Bible Church for construction of Sunday school classrooms, and plowing a garden for Elizabeth and Bill. When the deadline arrived, he prevailed upon Elizabeth to loan him the speech she had given in 1951 and had gifted David to present in 1955. *Good thing memories are short in the community of Joyce and no one remembered Demosthenes and the pebbles, and how perseverance brings success.*

We were proud of Mert's academic accomplishments and his persistence in studies. We were thrilled with his inventiveness and muscles on the farm. Yet, the slightest frustration could detonate an avalanche from his tongue. His periods of kindness and good-will were split apart by acts of anger and self-will. We expected the Divine Teacher would send more attention-grabbers, and prayed our son would take heed.

The summer after graduation, Mert was employed at Crescent and Agate Beach, as were others of our teens. This gave them access to launch their own fishing boat off the resort dock. On one blustery afternoon, Phil and Mert took out their unwieldy 13-foot wooden boat. They had barely begun their fishing adventure and cleared the eddy by Tongue Point when the water turned turbulent and waves began to break over the boat. The 5-horse Johnson engine couldn't counter the current and the boys were being forced toward the jagged rocks. The resort's 24-foot charter boat whizzed past them, but no one on board acknowledged their thrashing about. The two boys continued to flail against the wind and currents—Mert furiously bailing buckets of water while Phil, at the helm, aimed the boat into each wave and sped up when he could. Then he had to swing back into the trough before the bucking surf could break over the front and douse them both—all the while begging God to keep the gas from running out. Through twisting waves, forward and backward and sideways, they expended every ounce of energy in their fight for survival. Just as the engine was spluttering a death rattle, the skiff bumped past the jutting stones and into calmer waves. Phil dribbled gas into the tank, and they limped into shore. Mr. Taggart of the charter boat had seen them and called the Coast Guard for rescue, but Phil knew it might have been too late had God not intervened. Still, no turnabout for my son Merton.

The next lesson came during the summer of 1964 when Mert and Phil spied a massive antiquated D8 Caterpillar in a field set aside as a right of way for power lines. "I bet I could drive that Cat," Mert said.

Phil, wanting no part of the consequences, shook his head. "Not me," he said. "I'm leaving."

For an hour or more, Mert used the Cat to roll over a stand of young alders. Back and forth he roamed, clearing the land whether or not logging was in the best interest of the project. The sheriff came to our door. An observer had told the contractor that he'd seen the Corey boy on the Cat. Mert's restitution would be to watch the brush fires so all the men in the crew could have a few days off.

What a task—attempting to control those mountainous bonfires of logs and stumps and branches. At night Mert slept near the fires, sometimes without anyone to keep him company. During the daytime shifts when he and Phil were occupied at the beach resort, we all got in on Mert's recompense. The fires and hot spots could flare so quickly those of us watching had to haul water in the tank truck to keep the perimeter from spreading. (I must add a post-note: The Cat's owner was so impressed with our youngster's skills that—after the penalty had been completed—he hired Mert to assist in the logging operation.)

In the fall of 1965, Merton finally opened his heart to God. Upon his return from a Christian retreat sponsored by Seattle Pacific College, he told me of his encounter. "During the messages at the camp, God started hammering away at my facade. Shame and remorse for my sin and rejection of God overwhelmed me. I began to face the lie I'd lived since I was old enough to pretend—a sham designed to protect me from being preached at."

When moisture swelled in his eyes, I reached across the table to touch his arm. He continued. "As God gripped me, I replayed the part I had acted as a leader of the high school youth group. It was easy to parrot what I'd heard, easy to fool the pastors."

I nodded in comprehension as he added, "Other memories plagued me like the fear of drowning when pinned under the tractor, and the terror of being lost at sea in the little boat. I relived again the words of God's warning on both occasions: '*This may be your last chance.*'"

I clutched a hanky from my apron as I, too, remembered those close calls. He said, "I was mulling over my sinful behavior, phony living, and God's persistence as I headed home from the meetings. On the ferry I said, 'Okay God, I'm tired of running away. I'm done living for myself. Forgive my sins and make me a new person.'"

My son looked at me and said, "Mom, now all your children are in."

"Glory to God," flew from my lips.

Merton was changed. He showed a bit more patience with our three foster boys and greater tolerance for the grungy tasks of the farm. I illustrated the new Merton in the following letter to Arthur:

> Mert is cleaning the barn. And he is not fussing. Isn't that something? He said, "It's bad—the barn is bad enough, but not THAT bad." He's tackling other jobs— sixteen projects in one day—like fishing, butchering, roofing, burning a stump, spotting an elk, teaching Janice to drive, and more. There won't be much for you to do when you get home. Mert's on top of things here.....Love to you, Margaret

What would the future hold for Merton Henry, the iron-willed, steel-strong, and fix-it genius? I couldn't envision. I could, however, rejoice in the knowledge he was not out of the fold, but in—one-hundred percent in. God had a blueprint for his life and he would listen for the Master Builder to reveal it.

Even as I pondered those thoughts, we received the next answer to our prayer. Merton was on the way to Prairie Bible Institute.

--SEVEN--

To Prairie Bible Institute

How many of our children attended Prairie Bible Institute (PBI) in Three Hills, Alberta, Canada? I've backtracked and counted, coming up with fourteen: eight of our own and the spouses of six.

Why would our youth travel so far away to take classes at PBI? A little history reveals some clues. Prairie was founded in 1922 to teach young people the truths of the Bible and to prepare them for missionary work. The environment was protective and the rules strict—not significantly diverse from what our children were used to. In 1943, Hazel Bruck (Art's sister) and her husband Emil moved from Tacoma to serve on staff and their son Don started attending Bible school. An invitation from them opened the door in 1944 for Virginia to begin high school. In 1947, Marilyn joined them for her 10th grade. Virginia left Prairie after high school, but returned to Alberta to marry John McLennan whose parents were on PBI staff. Elizabeth started Bible school in 1951. Before the school year ended, she came home to help me after the birth of Janice, our tenth child. Marilyn completed both high school and Bible school.

Virginia and Marilyn were long gone from PBI when John enrolled in 1958. He knew he would be a missionary, and PBI trained missionaries. Eleanor followed in 1961 after attending one year at Seattle Pacific College (SPC). Phillip's route to Prairie required disentanglements and detours during tumultuous years, so I've given his route some scrutiny.

Phil had graduated from high school at Joyce in 1960, as had Eleanor. Both started out at Seattle Pacific College that fall. A month later, Phil wrote he was failing his classes—a school like SPC was not for him—and he had no clue what he wanted to be when he grew up.

He quit at Christmas, said goodbye to his girlfriend from high school, and drove with Marilyn and Allen to Denver. He started spring classes at Rockmont College and worked as custodian at a church. In time for the following year, Arthur and I delivered Phil's rickety motorcycle for the school commute. He wrote that the Colorado winter about killed him and that the idea of college was dumber than dumb. He stuck it out to the end of the year, then talked of transferring credit to Cascade in Portland, where John and Virginia were located. He was marking time, starting and stopping, and not finishing anything. That summer Arthur said, "Phillip, I have the assurance and witness of the Lord. You should go to Prairie."

To Phillip, those words were God's answer to his begrudged confession of a few months earlier, "God, if you want me to go to that ol' school, I will."

Phil wrote in his first letter from PBI of his surprise at being assigned to room with George Richardson, the brother of our son-in-law Bill. George had been an accomplice in resourceful nonsense for as long as the two boys had known each other. I went to the Lord with a librarian's catalogue of concerns. *Would Phil ever study? Would he cause trouble? Would he get booted?*

From Prairie, via the gossip vine, I began to hear of those boys' antics. They'd steal out to hunt on Wednesday or Thursday all night, and sneak their kill into the room. On one occasion, they hung the carcass of a porcupine outside the window in the freezing weather. The authorities told them such display of trophies was not permitted. Not to be dissuaded, the boys discovered a corner in the kitchen freezer where they stashed parts—including the tongues—of such critters as jack rabbits and coyotes.

It was against school rules for them to cook in their rooms, but they were allowed to connect an electric skillet in the laundry room. They ate each varmint, including a bobcat. If the idea of wild cat meat didn't make my stomach turn, imagine how I felt when I heard they'd tried a gopher! At least Phil admitted the rodent tasted like dirt. They were known to leave limburger cheese out in the open, knowing the odor would deter anyone who might check up on them and discover their cache of game.

I heard later, much later, a comment made by the Dean of Men who admired the originality of these boys. "They are the type of people who are best prepared to serve the Lord in unpredictable, perilous places. They find creative ways to solve problems and accomplish their goals."

In the summer of 1963, Phil had arrived home from his first year at Prairie when a call came from Marilyn: "Is there *any* way Phil can get to Denver and drive back with Debi and Shari and me? Allen has to finish up his school and pastoral obligation. I want—no, I *need*—to come home."

We had no money and Phil had no money. None of us had any money! So naturally Phil said, "Sure I'll go…I'll hitchhike."

A neighbor offered Phil a ride as far as Bremerton, and from there he headed off on foot, carrying $35 in his pocket. I can't guess how many times, day and night, I murmured, *Where is he now? Does he have anything to eat?* I could do nothing but wait and pray, until we received his account:

I caught a couple of rides, then was dropped in the middle of Montana. The night felt interminable as I hiked the deserted roads, and the nocturnal sounds of the prairie punctuated the growling of my empty stomach. I reminded the Lord of my whereabouts, and rejoiced in God's promise of protection. In the predawn hours, I saw a flicker of light in the distance. Hours later I arrived at a crossroads where a truck idled—as if waiting for me—with a driver who consented to drop me at a bus station in Wyoming. Fortunately, I'd spent no money on food and had just enough cash in my pocket to purchase a ticket to Denver. (*Phil Corey*)

A day later he and Marilyn drove 1500 miles straight through to our place with her kids, ages 6 and 4, plastered on top of a crammed-full back seat.

In the fall Phil returned to PBI and within the next two years, Marian and Merton joined him. The younger brother—who'd studied math and played basketball for two years at Peninsula Junior College in Port Angeles—was another cohort for capers at the strict establishment. The following letter arrived after a couple of months, the first part written by Mert:

Dear Mom and all,
I thought seeing as how you managed to find time to direct that long epistle to me, I might drop you a note. I went hunting Sat—got a pheasant. Phil, George Richardson, and other boys went deer hunting and got a 130 lb spike. Surely a nice looking deer. Things going well in studies, not as hard as Jr College. Tests are coming up and the paper on the Fall of Man is due. Just ate some of the deer liver—surely was tasty. (Don't say anything about the deer so that it won't get back up here. Please! It doesn't matter who knows down there.) Love, Mert

Phil's postscript on the letter followed:

> Dear Folks,
> I noticed the end of Mert's letter regarding the deer I shot. He sounded like it might be illegal, but it wasn't. The main reason we keep quiet is so we don't have too many freeloaders. So the less we have to tell others, the better. That deer was so fat that I should have thrown away the fat instead of putting it in the hamburger. You never see a deer like that at home.
> I got transferred from speaking in chapel this Monday morning because another senior wanted to get his sermon over with, and he wanted to help me out too. I wasn't prepared enough—but then I never am. Now I have to speak on Dec 20, just two days before we start for home. (You know how awful it is for me to prepare a talk and I'd get out of it forever if I could.) I must say my main interest, however, is in a connection from Vancouver to Snohomish. Say hi to everyone, Phil

Phil's interest was PBI student Darlene Howell of Snohomish, a town about three hours from our place. Writing about this romance has brought me to the subject of our youths' courting at Prairie Bible Institute, a high school and Bible school that didn't permit social mixing. In spite of having signed manuals bulging with regulations, Virginia, Marilyn, John, Phil, and Eleanor all discovered the persons of their choice. How did they do it under the raptor retinas—more commonly known as eagle eyes—of faculty entrusted with surveillance of students and enforcement of standards? To address that question, I have backed up in the timeline and added the voices of our children articulating their tales—so humorous I had to include the full script.

Here's Virginia to replay her surreptitious venture:

> One day in 10th grade I was walking to classes from the dorm at Prairie High School when John McLennan, an older student winked at me. Two girls saw the act and reported to the principal and the boys' dean of students. The dean reprimanded John by quoting Proverbs 10:10: HE THAT WINKETH WITH THE EYE CAUSETH SORROW. Then he stated, "John, a year from now that girl will be a bad taste in your mouth."
>
> On another occasion I was scheduled to play piano while John would lead the singing. Someone must have perceived there were fireworks between us, and the no-contact rules received a new clause: "A girl will lead singing with another girl at the piano, and a boy will lead with a boy."
>
> Glances and secret smiles were all we could get away with. Then, at the Jr/Sr Banquet, to my jaw-dropping amazement, John was ushered to the seat beside me. (Although separation was enforced in all other aspects of school, on this single occasion staff perceived that mixed seating would help students learn social skills. Students, though, weren't allowed to pick their partner.) Cat calls burst forth from John's buddies who wondered how he pulled it off. I didn't know until later that John had bribed a student leader into giving him the seat next to Virginia Corey. At this banquet, I had my first private words with John, "This looks like a put-up job to me."
>
> Well, it might have been a put-up job, but it worked. I gave John my address and we wrote to each other all summer. *(Virginia Corey McLennan)*

Virginia was the first of our daughters at Prairie, and we assumed she would be shielded from love across the *Great Divide* between girls and boys. I was perplexed when, at sixteen, she began receiving letters from John McLennan. What else could I do but read mail going both directions. To forewarn John, I noted on the corner of my girl's envelopes, *Censored by Mrs. A. W. Corey.* Today, that might seem an invasion of a teen's privacy, but not so in my 1946 perception. Virginia explained PBI fall-out from student letter-writing:

> During the next school year—my high school junior year—yet another rule was established: "High school students may not correspond with persons of the opposite gender during summer break."
>
> That summer, since John couldn't write me, I asked the Lord to let me see him. Oblivious of our mutual interest, Uncle Emil and Aunt Hazel Bruck invited John—a schoolmate of their son Don—to help them move to Prairie, where they had been on a one-year trial basis. They sold all their belongings in Tacoma, delivered goods to my parents and John to visit me. My fleece to God had been answered by my clueless, rule-bound aunt, and I knew John would one day be my husband.
>
> As a postscript to that visit in 1947, John loves to re-enact his first impression of the Coreys, "When I arrived, I couldn't believe all those kids running out the door. I blinked and I blinked, then concluded they must be going around the back and coming out again!" *(Virginia Corey McLennan)*

That summer, when John McLennan visited, he and our second daughter Marilyn catapulted into a contest to see who could be quickest and most clever at getting the goat of each other. They acted with more sibling rivalry than all of her birth siblings. It was out of this scenario Marilyn decided Prairie was for her.

Once settled in school, Marilyn wrote about the boys she'd seen and what she thought of them. After a few discards from her over-loaded rolodex of options, she settled on Allen Thompson.

Marilyn told all about it:

My interest in Allen Thompson kindled while we were attending high school. However, after graduation from Grade 12, I didn't return for Bible school. Allen prayed I'd come back the following year so he would know I was *The One*. His petitions were answered. When sentiments escalated, we devised methods to communicate. One was through matching the color of our clothes. When Allen saw the color I was wearing, he'd go to his room and put on a comparable shade. Eventually, to save him the need for quick changes, we got into a pattern: Monday-blue, Wednesday-wine, and Friday-red. If one of us didn't wear the matching pigment, the other prayed the issue would disappear by the next color-coded day. Another opportunity for connection across the *River Jordan* between men and women was during gratis (unpaid work to help cover school costs). My assignment at the print shop was next to the dorm where Allen lived. I would look up from my station to the window he kept open in my direction even in sub-zero weather. When he'd glance my way, I'd duck back to the job. I was horrified the day Les, his brother, poked his head out the window and waved at me! The communication was no longer clandestine and no longer possible. After that I watched from my basement dorm room hoping to catch Allen's eye in the midst of the hordes of students passing by.

When Allen, a stellar and rule-abiding student, was a Bible school senior he visited Mr. Maxwell, the Principal. "Since I'm about to graduate," he asked, "may I have permission to attend Marilyn Corey's birthday party? It's at the apartment of her sister Virginia and brother-in-law John McLennan."

Mercy, I was bursting inside! We were so shy, hardly knowing how to express what we felt. Didn't take long. When I wrapped my arms around his neck, he lost it...in the sweetest kiss. A second soon followed.

That August, we met in Carter, Montana, where Allen worked on a farm. One evening, while parked in a hundred-acre field of golden wheat sparkling under the full moon, Allen—his arm holding me close— asked me to marry him.

Soon after, we traveled to my home in Washington, and Allen became acquainted with the whole Corey tribe. During the visit, 10-year-old Eleanor followed us everywhere we went, snooping to see if we held hands or kissed. She followed up by mailing a postcard to Allen, *Ha. Ha. I know you are going to get married. Love, Eleanor (Marilyn Corey Thompson)*

Years later, our son John entered Prairie Bible Institute. He never wrote about girls—they weren't on his radar. In fact, his brother David once told him, "If you don't date, you'll probably never get married."

But John wasn't worried, knowing if God had a wife for him, she would show up and he would know. This is his story:

I was waiting tables in 1961, my junior year at PBI, when I first noticed Jeanette. I'd not paid attention to girls, instead had concentrated on learning the Word and preparing for missions. That day when I saw her, I felt something I'd never felt before and whispered under my breath, "This is nice."

In the summer both of us were on staff at Sammamish Bible Camp near Seattle. Our friendship grew as we discovered a mutual interest in Ethiopia as a place to serve.

After our first date my feelings for Jeanette were sealed. In the fall of our senior year at Prairie, I had to make every move count in order to see her. Timing was everything. Jeanette sang in the school choir and I practiced with the orchestra in another building.

During the next hour we both had accordion lessons in separate rooms of that building. I would position myself in the men's latrine and watch through the window. When she came my way, I'd fall in line about two or three steps behind and we'd climb the stairway together, perfectly paced and perfectly spaced. That way we wouldn't get apprehended for violating the no-contact rule. I never told Jeanette of my scheme, wanting to protect her if she were questioned. But I suppose she didn't feel too badly about seeing me either.

You couldn't get engaged while studying at Prairie, but the two of you could have an understanding—a pre-engagement agreement about which the faculty was aware and supportive. During the senior year, the couple could arrange for monthly appointments to see each other in the office of the ladies' dean. Seated behind a curtain on a couch, the pair would converse quietly, in hopes the hard-of-hearing dean could not eavesdrop.

It was in one of these meetings, I asked Jeanette to marry me. When she said yes, I kissed her. Right there in the dean's office...behind the curtain...I kissed my girl! We would have to keep our engagement secret until after graduation, but I knew God had brought that one person into my life.[8] *(John Corey)*

In 1961, the same school year John took interest in Jeanette, Eleanor entered PBI. She didn't write about boys—kind of a surprise to me. It was after she graduated and arrived at Seattle Pacific, she made connection with PBI classmate Ron Guderian. For that reason, I've saved their courtship for a later chapter.

Phil left for his first year at Prairie in 1962, traveling in the same car as Eleanor and her friend, Darlene Howell, both returning for their second year. Soon he was thinking up ways to see her at her home in Snohomish, a few hours from our place. I thought Darlene came from a classier family than ours and couldn't quite grasp her tolerance of his goofiness and of his clothes that smelled of fishing or hunting gear. So I wasn't exactly surprised to hear—at least on one occasion—her response to his tomfoolery, "Oh grow up, Phil."

Their relationship was sealed by the time she showed her own spontaneous rule-testing act when she was a senior and he, a junior.

Phil wrote:

> My gratis (unpaid) work was to store and deliver suitcases of the students when they arrived or prepared to leave—at beginning of the year, Christmas break, and end of the school term. One season, I dilly dallied on completing the task hoping to cross paths with my girl—Darlene Howell. Finally, I was climbing stairs in the girls' dorm when I saw her starting down that same stairwell. My heart took a leap and I wondered, *What can I say*? I needn't have worried, for when Darlene got to my step, she smacked a big kiss on my lips. I was flabbergasted into silence and beet red in the face as she flew past me.
>
> To this day, I don't know where she got the nerve to break the strict rules for which we had signed on the dotted line. Until then, we'd been a hundred percent conscientious in our behavior, and the best I'd ever done was to find her schedule and cross the blue-to-pink pathway to intercept with a smile and hi. Well, she outdid me, big time!
>
> "I didn't really break the rules," Darlene said later, "I followed the five-second rule; if it happened in fewer than five seconds, it wasn't really an infraction. On my clock I did the deed in two seconds maximum, so no worries!" *(Phil Corey)*

Thus our children creatively wooed would-be spouses at Prairie Bible Institute where laws of separation were designed to keep them free of distraction. At the same time, all were receiving Bible training with an integrated focus on missions. They were preparing for God to call them to places of adventure, poverty, and peril. They knew He would keep his Word: DO NOT BE AFRAID; DO NOT BE DISCOURAGED, FOR THE LORD YOUR GOD WILL BE WITH YOU WHEREVER YOU GO. And they knew they would be in good hands.

Students at Prairie Bible Institute, 1963
Back row: Darlene Howell, Phil Corey, Bill Reese, unidentified,
Front row: Ellen Morrison, Eleanor Corey, George Richardson

--EIGHT--

In good hands

God touched our offspring and they were primed to go. Even today, I am blessed to call to mind the number of our children—seven—and the places they went: Cuba, Dominican Republic, Ethiopia, Ecuador, Singapore, Colombia, Irian Jaya...to name a few.

It seemed as soon as I would get over saying goodbye to one family, another was packing trunks and barrels. My remember-to-pray list got longer and longer as my children and their little ones embarked for all corners of the globe. Neither they nor I could have anticipated the political and military war zones, isolation, diseases, and even death to which they would be exposed. I could only count on knowing they were in God's will and in His hands.

To share the impact of my offspring around the world and the endangerment they have faced, I've backed up to 1956. That's the year Marilyn and Allen Thompson set off for Cuba. Allen went to fill the role of dean at the Bible Institute (Los Pinos Nuevos) his father, Elmer, had established in 1929 to train national pastors, leaders, and missionaries. Allen's fit was perfect. He'd grown up as a Cuban and spoke their language, but he'd also studied at Columbia Bible College where he developed academic and ministry skills he could use to renovate the institute's philosophy and curriculum.[9] He and Marilyn would also be near Allen's brother, Les, and his wife, Mary, who were already established as radio missionaries.

Marilyn, my olive-skinned, black-haired daughter—looking more Latin than Allen—but without words to speak or ears to understand, prepared for the imminent delivery of her first child.

Within months of Debi's birth, rebels started taking over cities. Fighting filled the streets and the young Thompson families could hear explosions and gunshots. Ultimately, the government fell and the new regime began executing sympathizers of the former dictator Bautista. Arthur and I listened to conflicting radio reports and I begged God to send the little family home.

Two years later, Marilyn—still in Cuba!—gave birth to Shari. At the same time, Les's wife, Mary, flew to her hometown of Bellingham, Washington. While awaiting the birth of her third child, Mary became critically ill. When she died, her living baby was surgically delivered. Three little missionary kids had lost their mother. Such grief I could not comprehend.

Because of the revolution and dangers in Cuba, Mary and Marilyn had privately committed to take each other's children should need arise. In keeping with that promise, Mary's three boys (and Les part-time) went to live with Marilyn and Allen.

I fretted, *Oh my, five preschoolers, three years old or less. Mine were at least 15 months apart.*

Castro declared his control by dictatorship in 1960, and the missionaries—for their safety and for the protection of their national coworkers—were called home. We anticipated the arrival of our Thompsons including all five little ones in time for Christmas. Marilyn and Allen would spend a couple of years in the United States after which they would go to the Dominican Republic as missionaries. During that interval, Les married Carolyn and the boys went to live with them. For my daughter Marilyn and her little girls having to say goodbye to the little guys who'd been part of their family for two years triggered another crushing loss.

But what would become of Cuba?—a regime in cahoots with the Russians. Reports told that the international crisis was averted, but everyone knew the Cubans were in for catastrophic conditions under communism. Our children and grandchildren were safe, but our hearts sank in sorrow on behalf of those who were losing their land, their belongings, and their freedom.[10]

In 1965, John and Jeanette set off to Ethiopia. They had been married in 1962, shortly after graduation from PBI. From a camping honeymoon (John's idea), they entered school at The Bible Institute of Los Angeles (BIOLA) for missionary medical training. They were preparing for Africa with Sudan Interior Mission (SIM). Once they had their financial support lined up, we saw John, Jeanette, and one-year-old Melodie off in Seattle for Vancouver, BC. I noted in my journal:

> John and Jeanette are happy to go, and we are
> happy they are in God's will. But we will miss them.
> *(The diary)*

The young family traveled first by train across Canada to New York City. During the last leg of that ride, Melodie became severely ill with high fever, vomiting, and diarrhea. They rushed her to a New York hospital, where the attending doctor told them if they'd been delayed much longer the little one would not have survived. With medical care, she was soon back to her energetic self. In April 1965, the family boarded a Norwegian freighter for the six-week trip to Ethiopia. For nine months they focused on learning Amharic, the complex language of the Ethiopians, during which time Doreen (Reenie) was born. They settled in the village of Burji where God gave them a teaching and caring ministry. We waited eagerly for word from Jeanette whose letters could only be sent out of Burji every four to six weeks when the Missionary Aviation Fellowship

(MAF) plane arrived. Of course, that meant they also had four to six weeks of silence from our side of the world.

They had a third child, Nathan, who grew into a happy, curious little boy. We were heartbroken when word came that this little grandson, at 19 months, had died. Peanuts had lodged in his trachea, hindering the flow of air. Nathan struggled through the night and into the following day until a plane could land in their village. He was rushed to a mission hospital, but didn't survive the surgery. I couldn't comprehend the suffering of John and Jeanette and their little girls in this loss, but I had to trust God to understand and bring His comfort. Years later, we learned that one of the villagers, who'd also lost children, watched John and Jeanette through their grief. He said to John, "Now you understand us."

John and Jeanette spent nine years in village work and teaching, during which time Shari, Debbie, and Joycie were born. The family transferred to Dilla in 1975, just a day's drive from their oldest daughters at the Bingham Academy boarding school in Addis Ababa. By then, Ethiopia was already falling into turmoil. The communists ousted and imprisoned Haile Selassie, who died in jail. News reports reminded us of the carnage of communist takeovers in other parts of the world. We cried out for the millions of people losing their freedom, and prayed specifically for our children and grandchildren, "Keep our loved ones safe and bring them home."

Jeanette had to be shrewd in writing to us as mail was censored, but we understood they had bags packed in case of evacuation, and that most missionaries were already leaving. John knew his time of ministry would be limited, but his heart was burdened to leave behind Christian leaders who would remain strong through certain persecution. He taught and discipled committed nationals and spoke for gatherings of youth and elders who, more than ever before, were seeking to learn God's Word. John facilitated recordings of literate nationals reading—more like chant-singing—scriptures to their own melodies. These recordings would be shared so others could listen via hand-cranked cassette players until they too could sing the scriptures by memory. God allowed John and Jeanette an extension of more than a year from the time they were told by mission leaders to have their emergency supplies packed for instant exit.

While the couple continued strengthening the church, the children—during the school year—resided apprehensively within Addis Ababa, a city under siege. We didn't learn until after the family returned to the USA the trauma the children faced during many months in Bingham Academy as war raged on the streets outside the compound. Here are Jeanette's words:

> Our concern grew, not for ourselves, but for our four daughters at the academy which was located in an area of escalating violence. Near the compound was one of many execution points, and bodies of those who resisted the revolutionaries were sometimes left on the street as warnings. On the way to church one morning, our oldest daughter, Melodie, saw bodies of two men who'd been beheaded. Other times the girls would see trucks of armed communists, and even children, pointing guns as if they would shoot anyone in sight.
>
> An hour down country in Dilla, John and I were in a less volatile zone, so on occasion I was able to visit the girls at the school. On one such visit, during what seemed like a quiet time, I took my three youngest daughters and Shari's friend to purchase ice cream bars. Before we ever got to the store, a barrage of shots sent us scurrying out of sight into an alley. When the shooting ended, we discovered Debbie had an injury to her hand from a pebble that had ricocheted when bullets hit the ground. We were shaken, but how thankful I was for God's promises to PROTECT (US) FROM ALL EVIL AND TO GUARD (OUR) GOING OUT AND COMING IN.
>
> The school had prepared an underground emergency shelter for students and staff. When shooting would erupt, the two older girls, Melodie and Reenie, would slide from their upper story

> bedrooms down two flights of bannisters to crawl into the *safe* place, where they would huddle until the sounds of warfare ceased.
>
> Sometimes warning didn't come quickly enough. I was torn to the core when I learned that—as a battle broke out and bullets flew over the compound—our elementary-age daughters Shari and Debbie had hidden in terror at the back of a closet. They were sobbing when the staff found them. Shari wrote to me, "Mom, I just can't stop crying." *(Jeanette Corey)*

When only a handful of missionaries remained in the entire country, and the school would have to close, God had made it clear to John and Jeanette it was time to leave—that their work was done.

We were so relieved to get word in the summer of 1978, they were on their way out of communist-ruled Ethiopia. Our son, his wife, and their daughters, Melodie, Reenie, Shari, Debbie, and Joycie, left behind a marker where little Nathan was buried, and tore themselves away from the nationals with whom they had shared the gospel of Christ. They would take the following year for respite and recuperation in a home near Seattle. When John said they were ready to go again, SIM assigned them to Liberia, where God is now giving them fruitful ministry.

We back up to catch Phil and Darlene who began their missionary venture by applying to serve with West Indies Mission (later named World Team) in 1966, soon after they were married. A year later—following the birth of Mark—they left for language school in Texas and on to the Dominican Republic (DR). *How long before I see them again?* I wondered, as I always did when my own left our homeland. During their subsequent years overseas, Melanie was born, and Phil and Darlene adopted Tim and Jenny.

In the DR, Phil managed a mission conference facility that functioned both as a center for retreats and a place to reach young people with the Gospel. He seemed a perfect fit for the camp option…perhaps not for preaching assignments. I remembered how hard for him to prepare and give messages in English, so I was convinced preaching in Spanish would be the most difficult test in missions he would face. Not so!

Little Jenny was four years old when, on Nov 13, 1982, we received a call from the DR. Phil tried to speak, but was so broken up he could scarcely relate what happened. Apparently, he had seen Jenny some fifty feet away when he and the two older children climbed in the drivers' side of the truck. Out of their sight, Jenny had darted back to jump onto the passenger running board, but couldn't hold on. Embedded in Phil's memory was the sensation that he had run over a bump he knew had not been there. A national doctor and a young friend, Josue, sprinted toward the child. Blood oozed from her ear and nose, her head was squished out of shape, and her teeth were askew. Josue held her in the back of the doctor's Volkswagen Bug with Phil at their side, as the panic-stricken doctor lurched the stick shift car to the Dominican hospital. Darlene, her own being in a turmoil, murmured to Jenny, "Now that was scary, wasn't it?"

Jenny nodded yes, bringing an inch of hope to those around her.

In the ER, the attendants used Phil's pocket knife to cut off Jenny's shirt and sent the parents from the room. That's when Phil found a phone. Arthur prayed immediately over airwaves. With confidence, he responded to our son, "God has heard."

Additional information came in a letter from Darlene:

> Other friends of ours, Dr. Renee Alvarez and his wife, Vicki, rushed to the hospital. In Jenny's room, Renee said, "I see the tire marks on her body and you, Phil, tell me you felt the bump. So I believe it happened. The only thing I can say is, God lifted the truck so the full weight did not roll over her."
>
> Vicki too was astonished. "My prayer worked; they were finally able to insert the IV."

I replied, "You know I've always said, 'you, too, have a hotline to heaven. Your prayers are just as good as mine.'"

We were rejoicing in the smallest victory when the attending national physician came to offer his services to explore—via scalpel—what internal damage might have occurred. He said reconstructive surgery for her face would be necessary...if she lived. Renee motioned and mouthed to Phil, "Don't do it!"

Defying all the medical alarms, Jenny's face almost immediately regained its round shape and X-rays showed no internal bone or organ damage. We are so thankful to God for the miracle of Jenny's life... Love, Darlene

The child would receive no exploratory or reparative surgery. Over time, her nose, ear, wandering eye, and broken jaw would mend. God had answered the prayers of many around the world. Arthur and I have seen Jenny since that accident, and can attest to the fact that God has given her full health and a sweet spirit.

The next to fly overseas were Eleanor and Ron with their oldest two, Jeff and Joy. To catch their journey I revisited 1964, the year of our daughter's graduation from Prairie Bible Institute and her summer tours with the choir and trio. In the fall Eleanor entered Seattle Pacific College as a junior (she'd completed one year prior to PBI and had been given a year of academic credit from Bible school). Classes were underway when she showed up at our door in an itsy bitsy Renault she had purchased for $200—plus a little—for commuting to classes. At the wheel was Ron Guderian, about whom she had tipped us. They had known each other at Prairie, but apparently, he didn't pay much attention to her attempts at being an eye catcher across the *Gazing Strip*. On this first visit to our place, most of Ron's hours were spent working on the Renault—a flimsy car that returns in a later chapter—and whispering with Eleanor late at night in the kitchen. Ron fit right into the fraternity on the job sites, for he, too, had grown up with creative skills and a hardworking farm ethic. He, however, had come from a one-person-talks-at-a-time family and seemed ill at ease around the boisterous bunch of jabber-all-at-once Coreys. I'd see him sitting off to the side and wonder whatever in the world he was thinking.

I knew what Ron was thinking about a year later when he and Eleanor took Arthur and me to dinner at Traylor's restaurant, a place where she had once waited tables. Yet he spoke of nothing significant all the way through multiple courses and dessert, and even past the desertion of the place by other patrons. I noticed our daughter trying to prompt him to get to the point, until finally he asked permission for marriage.

In December 1966, Ron and Eleanor were married at Emmanuel Bible Church in Seattle. She taught school in the region until their son Jeff was born in 1968. After Ron graduated from Seattle Pacific College in 1967, he continued his studies to earn a PhD in biochemistry at the University of Washington, followed by a residency in clinical pathology in San Francisco. During the two years Ron and Eleanor were in California, Joy was born. The family attended Redwood Chapel in Castro Valley where they met missionaries from HCJB Radio in Ecuador. They were assured the ministries of this organization were a close fit to Eleanor's musical skills and Ron's medical preparation.

In 1973, Ron and Eleanor visited HCJB in Quito, Ecuador, and the mission hospital in Shell Mera, leaving with us their two children—Jeff (5) and Joy (2)—for a month. (At the time, I'd forgotten how exhausting it was to have full responsibility for little ones, and Arthur didn't see a reason to let up on his ministerial duties, so we trucked the two active youngsters along. Or at Jeff's request, and for our own reprieve, we dropped them at Elizabeth's place to play with the cousins, David and Karen Richardson)

Ron and Eleanor returned from their trip to gather financial backers and to pack for language school in Costa Rica. In 1974, we transported their troupe and trunks to the train depot in Seattle for the first leg of their trip overseas. Once again, I was faced with good-byes, and once again, got a knot in my chest as they

Street Scene in Ecuador, 1976

boarded. The battle had been won many years earlier when I released my children and my grandchildren into God's hands for wherever He would lead them. But still, the pain of parting was real.

For more than fifteen years, we have poured over letters that tell of Ron's *Dr.-Livingston-I-presume*[11] endeavors. We have read of his medical and dental caravans; his diagnosis and treatment of tropical diseases; his investigation of the use of shock as a first-aid measure for venomous bites; and other too-scientific-to-name medical breakthroughs.[12] Ron's presentations during furloughs are not to be missed—nor are Eleanor's vocal mini concerts. We are thrilled that our daughter has found in Quito a place of service through music, whether teaching in the high school, directing the radio choir, or leading a musical featuring the voices of Jeff and Joy and other children at HCJB. I, of course, am overjoyed when they and their Quito-born child, Janell, arrive for a few weeks of furlough.

In 1975, Merton and Debbie left for their overseas ministry. A journey together had kicked off a decade earlier—in the summer of 1967 after Mert had finished his junior year at PBI. He was working at Crescent Beach Resort—the same location where high school student Debra Jean Thompson (Debbie) was helping in the home of the resort owners. Fireworks of romance kindled, leaving me to wonder if this attraction would lead the young couple to the altar. Mert returned to PBI for his senior year, graduating in the spring of 1968.

In the fall of 1968, Debbie left for PBI and Merton enrolled at Seattle Pacific College (SPC). He planned to complete a degree in math for which he had earlier studied two years at Peninsula College in Port Angeles. A few weeks into the term at SPC, Mert quit, informing me that the academic institution didn't suit him, nor did the idea of teaching arithmetic. He had met the Lord—that was enough.

Merton knew the military draft board would call him, and within weeks the word arrived—Merton was classified as 1-A (first-to-be-called). A few months later, on March 11, 1969, he received his summons to report for induction at Fort Lewis.

What a cultural shock he experienced at the base—filthy conditions of the camp kitchen where he was assigned, ungodly lifestyles of the other inductees, and his own struggle to give testimony of faith.

When the boot camp was complete, Arthur and I took Debbie to the award ceremony. Merton had come out highest in his Physical Fitness Test, and had won two special awards along with a pin for rifle skill. The ceremony was thrilling, and our buttons strained with pride over our son's achievement. In the midst of the celebration, my soul was burdened for all the men in uniform, many of whom would be sent to the front lines of Vietnam. For months we had been drawn to—yet dreading—the news which listed the number of American casualties in a war dragging on and on without solution. My pledge that day was to intercede daily for each soldier to be ready to meet the Lord, should he come up against forces of mortality.

Merton was trained in Virginia for airframe repair mechanics in preparation for Vietnam. He would be a support to the military effort rather than a soldier packing a gun—a gift to all of us who loved him. Mert was given a month leave in the fall—time to see his girl at PBI in Three Hills. Then our son was gone.

Soon after his arrival in Vietnam, word came an airbase had been hit and several killed or injured. I wrestled, *Could it be the one where Merton is repairing helicopters?* Praise God!—not his airbase, not Merton. He didn't sound concerned for his safety...so I carried the burden for him, especially when I learned he was assigned armed guard duty to protect the base.

Our son sent descriptions of his mechanical repair work and his opportunities to practice flying a helicopter. He wrote of bureaucratic activities around base, as included in his letter to Janice on the occasion of her graduation in 1970 from high school:

> ...We just finished our big inspection and did very well from what I hear. Surely should have for all the work. You couldn't believe the foolishness to get ready—a lot absolutely ridiculous. But the Army is noted for how much crazy stuff they can make a guy do. If you want to have to work for a living, join the Army and come to Nam. Now that the inspection is over, maybe we'll get a day off once in a while like they promised.
>
> ...Love, Mert

Merton tried to keep his tone light when writing about circumstances near his base. But we knew countless refugees were fleeing—many in overloaded boats that sank, or across explosive-mined land, or into the torturing hands of the enemy. After one of my nights of restless apprehension, Arthur phoned an organization to offer housing for displaced Vietnamese. Nothing came of our call, though I kept pleading, "God have mercy on those poor souls and on our world."

After completing his duty in Vietnam, Merton was stationed in Alaska. In October 1971, he received honorable discharge. Meanwhile Debbie had taken classes for two years at PBI, after which she earned a degree in Practical Nursing in Port Angeles. In April 1972, the couple was married at Joyce Bible Church. Soon after the wedding, they were accepted by Missionary Aviation Fellowship (MAF). They would leave for assignment as soon as they could raise funding—$900 a month. To me, the amount sounded impossible…and it would have been without God prodding his people! From Ethiopia, John wrote a letter pledging a donation for passage to the field, although Mert and Deb had been regularly sending funds for John and Jeanette. Such a blessing it was to watch our children, including those on mission fields themselves, supporting each other.

In January 1976, Merton and Debbie left for language school in Costa Rica in preparation for Colombia. Arthur added their photo to the world map on the wall of the living room—alongside the other missionary photos, so we would be nudged during devotion time to bring their safety and service to the Father. My son was soaring over mountains and jungles and rivers in a STOL Cessna 180…or he was repairing planes for other pilots to fly over those same places. I devoured Debbie's reports of manning the radio in sweltering heat, while Mert delivered missionaries and goods to their bases, or took nationals in need of medical attention to health facilities.

After six years, Merton and Debbie moved into our basement while they created a chalet in "The Rat Hole" above Eden Valley. In 1984, they spent another year with MAF in Indonesia, then returned home to live. Now Mert is a pillar at Joyce Bible Church where he serves as teacher, worship leader, and builder. Is there need for construction of classrooms, or for an upgrade of facilities? Merton is on top of it. In the community, he and Debbie minister to all with whom they come in contact and—for Arthur and me— Mert's help is only a phone call away. As I might have mentioned before, never have I known such a hardworking, dynamic, ingenious, and resourceful servant of God…and of humanity.

Not only do the missionaries face challenges on their respective fields, they and their children often encounter unsettled and unpredictable conditions during furloughs (or home assignments—

the updated title of the time when they share their work and reunite with those they've not seen for years). These furloughs can be as stressful as their lives overseas. Yet, since they don't complain, perhaps I'm allowed to grumble on their behalf. They live out of jam-packed suitcases. They sleep in slop-and-slosh waterbeds and lumpy-squeaky hideabeds. They borrow cars that may have once smugly assisted their masters, but have reached beyond their time-to-be-retired years. On more than one furlough, Ron and Eleanor borrowed a large sedan—Big Bomb, they called it—with a faulty driver's window that would crash down into the door. To retrieve what had disappeared, the driver had to stop, climb out, and pull up the glass, only to anticipate its collapse at the next bump.

Then there was the station wagon Phil and Darlene borrowed for their cross-country furlough trip from Florida to Washington. This loaner blew its engine in the middle of barren Wyoming, leaving the couple and their children Mark, Melanie, and infant Tim stranded at the side of the road until strangers took charge. In this case, God gave miracles on every level—rides, repairs, and money for food and fares, until they reached a church destination in Montana.[13]

My family tells me the most difficult adjustment for missionaries and especially for their children is the return to the culture of their homeland. The parents may perceive that people expect them to be *perfectly* holy. The missionary kids (MKs) feel out of place, as if they are from another planet. These youth, sometimes called third-culture kids, can relate to multiple cultures and speak more than one language, yet they don't feel they belong anywhere—not their parents' home country, nor their adopted land. They feel conspicuous for what they wear, for what they say, and from whence they have come. One missionary explained the phenomenon like this, "MKs often flounder like fish out of water seeking to find an environment where they can breathe and friends with whom they can relate."

No matter where my missionary families find themselves—on the field where the needs of people call to them, or on furlough where we and others engage them in our services—I know they need the Father's care. I've gone to prayer meetings whether I felt up to it or not, so I could share their concerns. Praying and crying—which some called "craying"—is what I have done. I have missed being with the young families when new babies came, missed holding the newborns, and missed easing the adjustment of the new mothers. I have reproached myself for forgetting birthdays and anniversaries, but have labelled RED LETTER the days when the aerograms—thin paper that is folded to form an envelope for sending by international airmail without enclosure—have arrived, or when a ham radio operator has phone-patched to us a voice from afar.

Construction of Mission Hospital in Ecuador, 1991
Team Director Merton (front center).

These children, whose calling has taken them overseas, are buttressed by siblings located in our homeland. The commission to share the love of Christ also motivates them, and these North American family members support their sibling missionaries with finances, serve alongside for weeks or months, or gather helpers and equipment for special work team projects. Arthur and I are humbled in gratitude to God for selecting us to parent such an entourage of faithful stewards.[14]

Of my numerous other relatives, the journal is brimming, and I wouldn't know where to begin nor what to write...except to say: I know all of my loved ones are in good hands. When they are in dangerous situations, or when they make choices that lead them away from God, my soul churns like the ocean currents pulsing through Deception Pass on their way to Puget Sound. The Heavenly Father has never forsaken them and never will. My constant role— the part that diffuses the internal tides of pressure—is to commit each one to Him, to commit and commit and commit...

This reminds me of how often my husband has had to commit *me* to the Lord. Not because of danger I've faced, but because—at times—I've become disagreeable, disgruntled, dis...whatever. So, while I have focused above on the role of incubating and un-nesting my brood, it's time to review the internship of serving with my spouse. Such a long practicum it's been! I'm sure you'll come to the same opinion as I have—in this school of acquiescence, I am a slow learner. But, by God's grace, I've chosen to remain in class.

PART III

TO BE A HELPMEET
(1960—1970)

--NINE--

Arthur was right...I admit it

After my young flew from the nest, Arthur expected me at his side whenever he was ready to travel the itinerate ministry road. I knew I should be willing, yet I often backpedaled. When I could find no way out, I would pack my bags of submission...with the speed of a sloth. After the trip, I'd have to acknowledge that God had led my husband. Cases-in-point are the following excerpts taken from random dates in the diary:

> ...Arthur said, "Let's go." I didn't want to, but—after stewing awhile—I conceded. Know what?—God blessed me and a whole lot of other people too.
>
> ...We had to take a different route than planned. *Hate to show up anywhere without calling.* A detour made it necessary, and the couple was glad to see us. "God sent you," they said.
>
> ...I wondered what was going through my husband's mind. We went—against my better judgment—and God met the needs of many.

...The children got along okay in my absence—guess my husband knew what the Lord would have ME do, even when I didn't.

...Our house was full of bodies. We must have been 40 kinfolk and others when Arthur answered the phone and said to distant relatives who were headed our way, "Of course, come."

I argued, "There is indeed an overabundance of confusion already."

My words were wasted—these additional half dozen mouths to feed were only miles away. In truth, I did enjoy the visit and once again, the Lord multiplied the loaves and fishes. *(The diary)*

Margaret and Arthur, 1951

For a more detailed example, I revert to 1964. Arthur was contemplating a voyage to the Dominican Republic to assist Marilyn and Allen Thompson who'd settled there and were preparing for a nationwide evangelistic campaign. Each time Art entered his virtual closet, he received assurance God's plan was for *us*, not solely for him. Yet, I balked. In my imaginings, an endeavor of such magnitude felt like a trip to Mars, and people hadn't even gone to the moon yet. *How could I possibly go so far away? To a Spanish-speaking country where civil unrest is common and safety not assured?*

I wasn't a bit concerned for myself, but quite distressed about those who depended on me. We had two young daughters: Marian, 17, and Janice, 12. Both were at vulnerable ages and stages. Arthur maintained others would look out for these daughters with equal or greater vigilance. We were also responsible for the two boys, Edward and Stacey, who had remained after Ricky was placed in the Vancouver Boys Academy. If we traveled to the Dominican Republic, these preteen boys would stay at our friends or relatives, and I worried there would be reports of trouble. "What about *them*?" I stewed.

Arthur said—and I agreed—Edward and Stacey were taking more responsibility for their attitudes and behavior. In fact, they were doing so well, we'd let them fix up a cabin where they could sleep, allowing them opportunity for independence from supervision. The two added their enthusiasm to yard games with our grandchildren, and it hadn't been long since we had watched Ed and Stacey and a whole batch of McLennan and Richardson kids play Kick the Can—a running and hiding activity that had been a favorite pastime on our farm for two generations. That day the silence of kids disappearing behind trees and stumps, followed by their squeals while racing for the can, caught my attention. Suddenly Edward swooshed from his hiding place and kicked the can—the wrong can—the can filled with nails and water. Pain spread across his face, but he assured us he would be alright. Seems he limped for some time after that, but he never complained.

The boys went with us to church and indicated they wanted to follow God's way. Edward especially had a smile and sincerity that touched me, and I sometimes set aside a piece of pie just for him. Arthur was confident these youngsters would not create problems while we were away for a few weeks. "But," I stewed under my breath, "who will look out for my mother?"

I had to *own up*, Mother Edith was my biggest concern. She had been in the Port Angeles Convalescent Center for more than a year, and was ill. *What if she grew worse while we were so far away? What if the nurses called for me to come? What if life-altering decisions had to be made? What if...?* Multiple what-ifs flooded my thoughts whenever Arthur reminded me—with appropriate verses about choosing to trust God—he was waiting for my answer. *What if she died?* At the thought of losing my mother, a railroad train of memory assembled itself in my head. I circled back to 1935, when Art received God's call to preach. Mother started listening to my dad and other relatives who disparaged my husband for taking me and our young ones on what skeptics said was a "reckless preaching pursuit." I remembered my heartbreak when my father died in 1938, soon after our move to Port Angeles. When we returned to Tacoma for the funeral, emotions on all sides were raw, not only because of the loss, but because of the unsettled breach. We excused ourselves from the tension to return to Joyce and the travail of winterizing our newly purchased structure—the original Ramapo Grange Hall wind-and-rain tunnel. Separation and time soothed the hurt, and we visited my mother every year or two, either returning to Tacoma for the birth of a baby, or taking with us a new child for her to meet. She welcomed each one—though I know she couldn't comprehend the frequency of their births.

More railroad cars of nostalgia were added to my mental locomotive. In 1954, we constructed a little house for Mother and she moved to our farm. At the time, our three oldest were gone, the next six were in school during the day, and Janice was the toddler who received extra attention from her grandmother. Most days the grandmother of my youngsters would sit in her front window, view activities on the farm, and report observations such as:

> ...I couldn't believe Phil and Mert were doing farm chores in their white band uniforms?

...I didn't know what to do when I saw Merton leave the gate open and the cows got out. I was afraid they'd go on the highway.

...Marian started a snowball fight with Merton and got the worst of it. Why doesn't she learn?

...See how nice David looks when he is cleaned up.

...I can see Delilah (the cow) is having an awful case of diarrhea. She should have a sitz bath[15] before anyone tries to milk her.

...Margaret, I don't know how you manage. There were so many cars coming in I lost track. How many did you feed last night? Most stayed the night, didn't they. Well I surely hope they helped pay for the food. *(The diary)*

In those days, I would repeatedly cross the yard to visit Mother. Arthur checked in as well—fixing her radio, repairing her heater, or changing a light bulb. She liked to hear of his travels and what God had said to him. But she also wrote to my sister and my cousin, telling them she couldn't understand how God would send him off when I was left with so much to do and so many mouths to feed.

Many years later, as I read one of her letters to a cousin of mine, I realized Mother had come to accept Arthur's ministry. Her words brought a smile to my face and overdue comfort to my soul:

Dear Naoma,

I just don't know how to answer your questions about Arthur. I feel he is on a level above us, and can't be judged by how we feel. He is doing far more good in this world than either you or I—that I know. Certainly not you nor I would have had the faith to cast everything on the Lord. He is wanted in so many places and it's a great strain on him. Then he works so hard here on the place.

He told me Allen asked him if he would consider going to S. Carolina. Arthur said if he felt the Lord calling him, he would leave everything. He told Allen he feels he (Art) couldn't help pastor a church, for you have to keep peace there. Arthur isn't one to keep peace at the expense of what he thinks is right. Better not mention this in an open letter. I think he is on a campaign to get me to believe as he does. Often Marg is surprised at what he tells me.

Made me chuckle when he said the sun was shining because he asked God for good weather so he could plant the garden.

Love, Your Aunt Edith

Mother's legs were crooked and stiff and lame from arthritis, and she only allowed us to bring her across the yard a few times for birthdays or Christmas. She fussed how none of her clothes fit, and how she needed to go on a diet, or exercise to take inches off—at 80-some years, no less! She insisted the girls and I weren't to buy or sew anything she didn't ask for, and we weren't to clean her house or put things away. I knew her independence was not to be trifled with.

My train of memory continued to stretch until it had connected logging trailers to sleeping cars to engines. There was my insomnia of 1963 when Mother developed pneumonia and had to be hospitalized. There was spring cleaning of her house in the fall, and dumping the special food she'd saved until rotten. When I questioned her, she confessed, "I knew it was spoiled but I couldn't reach it and didn't want to tell you."

We revamped her kitchen and installed electric heaters in preparation for her homecoming. One complication after another kept her in the hospital until the medical authorities sent her to the Campbell House Convalescent Center, where she remained. I visited her day after day, at least whenever a kind soul would drive me—*a nagging reminder of how foolish of me not to have a driver's license.*

As the memories of those years crescendoed to a train-on-the-trestle roar in my brain, I finally told Arthur how I really felt about leaving the country. "Mother will be alone. Our grown kids are so busy with their own families, they don't have time to visit her. I fear she will be discouraged and depressed, and I won't even be able to call her from so far away."

Soon after I had stated my rationale, Arthur came in from working at the saw mill, his face ashen. He told me how he was spared from a mechanical accident that might have killed him. Shock reverberated through my spirit. Had I not been pushing the brakes, by then we would have confirmed the trip. We would have contacted relatives for stops across the country, would have booked our flight from Miami to the Dominican Republic, and would have begun to pack our bags...all except for my fears and inability to trust God. *What if Arthur had been maimed, or worse?*

"Okay," I said, as he sat down to lunch, "You are right. I will go."

--TEN--

To the regions beyond

January 1966. Arthur's travel diary began with Psalm 32:8:

> I WILL TEACH THEE AND LEAD THEE IN THE WAY THAT
> THOU SHALT GO. I WILL GUIDE THEE WITH MINE EYE.

Whereas in my log were these words:

> Tears and prayer as we say goodbye to Mother in
> the Campbell House.

We started our missionary assignment in David's new Rambler with his gas card in hand. As we crossed the United States, Arthur had a message for each contact along the way—at the service stations, at cafés, and with our relatives. His word of encouragement, challenge, or confidence sprang from discernment of the person's need, or from a comment made in passing. A muscular African American stopped his mechanical work to ask questions, and a Shell station attendant wanted to know more about Jesus…for example.

We stayed overnight with people we knew, or we looked for hotel rooms—the cheapest in town, usually around $5.00. One night as we tried to sleep in a rooming house—dirty and foul smelling and buzzing with mosquitos—Arthur said, "This is proper missionary training."

His suggestion was not worthy of comment, so I changed the subject, "Why aren't there more places where a person can buy coffee for 20 cents?"

The Rambler gave us trouble, but it wasn't the roadster's fault. Arthur had forgotten what David told us about a fifth gear and, by the time we arrived in Florida, we'd overworked the fourth gear. We limped into a shop and left the Rambler for repairs. "Such an inconvenience," I grumbled.

We took the first train to Miami but were too late for our scheduled flight out. Later we recognized the disruption to us had allowed for God's appointments. There was Martin, the porter on the train whose heart was lonely; a Cuban book store owner who had known my brother Herbert Phenicie in Cuba; and the Sunday morning preacher who said, "At 60 years and past you get your best work done."

Aha!—we were singled out as prime age for God's service. We rescheduled our flight, and were soon on the way to the island country of the Dominican Republic (DR).

Scenes to which my north-western eyes were unaccustomed welcomed us—beggars pressing for a coin, airport workers expecting tips, coffee-brown barefoot kids playing ball in the street and in the fields, packs of barking dogs, closed bakeries, and empty grocery stores. On the main road out of the airport, we watched a funeral procession of imported laborers from Haiti—the tears, the wailing, the cross, the shaking of the coffin up and down. I thought, *Oh, that they might know the victory over death in Jesus Christ.*

We had situated our suitcases when Allen and Arthur left for the Evangelism-in-Depth meeting. Arthur was awestruck listening to our son-in-law preach in smooth Caribbean Spanish, the language he'd learned as a missionary child in Cuba. When it was Arthur's turn, he had to communicate through an interpreter. His frustration was palpable in his words below:

> The interpreter was tops but I was bottoms. My words were short and simple and his were many and complex.
>
> We have been many places and met many people, but we are never free of the language barrier. I feel like Zechariah must have felt when he didn't believe the angel's word and was stricken dumb.
>
> It's humiliating to admit I was more useful holding up the sound system speakers in a mighty windstorm than speaking God's words. *(Arthur Corey)*[16]

Arthur persisted in studies and practice, but still requested his nine-year-old granddaughter, Debi, to translate when he went to witness to Evi, the neighbor. Arthur returned home to report that this man had accepted the Lord, and everyone rejoiced—everyone that is, except his wife, Cessie. She had a queenly fit: royal enough to require a tranquilizer injection to quiet her. Praise God, Evi was born into the Kingdom and Cessie's time will come…we are certain.

Also unnerving—besides Arthur's hampered-by-translation preaching—was a gastric affliction that hit. In his words:

> There were attacks on us that are hard to relate, so personal and powerful and appalling, I was bewildered. In the middle of the night I awakened to cramps that sent me running to the bathroom. Worst purging in my entire 61 years. As I suffered through many hours, the song rang in my head, *Must I be carried to the skies on flowery beds of ease while others sought to win the prize and sailed through*

bloody seas? No, I must fight if I would win. Increase my courage Lord. I'll bear the cross and endure the pain, supported by Thy Word.[17] *(Arthur Corey)*

I, in decades of marriage, had never seen Arthur in such misery. He couldn't work on building or repair projects with Allen, nor could he preach. Marilyn and I were likewise on the bathroom marathon, but she was also lame with backache. I was glad to be an extra pair of hands in the house and a grand-sitter for Debi and Shari. Good thing the family spoke English for I couldn't even say a dozen words in Spanish. Oh, and the dog—the dog knew English. That was a relief, because Marilyn's helper—who worked alongside me—didn't.

We'd been with Marilyn and Allen and the girls for more than two months, and our infirmity had somewhat abated, when Arthur revealed our departure date. I whispered: *Hallelujah!* While I was thinking of home, Art was filled with a sense of assignment-accomplished. He wrote:

I WILL PRESERVE THY GOING OUT AND THY COMING IN FROM THIS TIME FORTH AND EVEN FOREVERMORE. And so closes a great experience of the grace of God, though we trust the continuing promise: THE LORD WORKING WITH THEM AND CONFIRMING THE WORD, WITH SIGNS FOLLOWING. Amen *(Arthur Corey)*

We flew back to hosts in Miami and caught up on home news in letters sent from Washington. The next day, we boarded the train to Ocala, Florida, where we collected the repaired Rambler. The head mechanic charged us $65 for the work and nothing for storage, saying he was blessed to know us. Then, after a week on the road, overnights with relatives, and one nice motel—no infested ones—we drove into our yard. How grateful I was to discover Mother improved in my absence. And there was no fallout from having left our daughters and Edward and Stacey in the supervision of others. God had answered.

As a post-it note, my human nature hasn't changed all that much in the 20 years since this first missionary journey. Not long ago when Arthur said "the light is green," I replied, "I want to be sure this is God's assignment, not just your itchy feet."

How blessed I am God's love and forgiveness are central to all His promises. He never allows more heat on the pressure pot of my life than He gives the peace I need and the strength to endure.

Addressing endurance—one pokey-to-arrive provision was a test of endurance for the entire clan. Even for Arthur, though I'm not sure he would fess up to the emotion.

--ELEVEN--

All these things—wheels

B ack in the thirties, after my relationship with the Lord had been secured and my accord with Arthur clarified, God began to fulfill the Word: SEEK YE FIRST THE KINGDOM OF GOD AND HIS RIGHTEOUSNESS, AND ALL THESE THINGS SHALL BE ADDED (Matthew 6:33).

All these things—even cars! The cars I write about are an example of the blessings of God—not always what we ask for, but what He chooses to give. They may not be adequate for a burgeoning family and may not always take us where we plan to go, but they always deliver us to the people the Father has prepared.

The history of our vehicles began with an early 1920s square top that took us from Tacoma to Port Angeles to Joyce. The family was small and all of us fit inside—since there were no rules about seat belts and car seats. Some of us remember a Whippet and a bumper-seat coupe of the early 40s, both of which required more than one trip to move everyone. After that season, we count the years when we had no car at all and could move no one. The children and I were shy to ask for rides, so we stayed home—even though we wanted to go. Arthur felt no shame, however, in walking the road until he got a ride. He often told people the lack of wheels was a blessing. "If God called me to travel, He provided not only a destination but also a driver's seat companion who needed a pastor-in-commute. During those trips there were souls who met the Lord."

In 1950, we inherited my cousin's '31 Chevy, which spent more of its existence in repairs than on the road. But when functional, it would hold the whole tribe plus six extras piled on top of each other and behind the seats. In 1953, we purchased a neighbor's '41 Plymouth Coupe that held three in the two-person front, a child standing behind, and—for short trips—the rest, along with a dog, in the trunk which was left open for ventilation.

'41 Plymouth Coupe, 1953
(Center front-the author at age 10)

In 1958, we became the owners of a '51 Chevrolet Station Wagon—the answer to my prayers for a wagon with lots of space. By then the older kids had departed the premises, but younger ones still needed to get to music and sports events or wanted to practice for drivers' tests.[18] We used the station wagon to move Arthur's mother, Anna Corey, into a nursing home and to move our belongings from the farmhouse across the yard to the Big House. We drove this vehicle until it succumbed to *organ* failure.

'52 Station wagon, Phil and Mert, ca.1960

Of the other leftovers we received from whomever and wherever, one rattletrap in particular was my nemesis—Tin-can Renault mentioned earlier in connection with Eleanor and husband-to-be, Ron. I can't count the number of trips during which that one left us stranded and unable to get to people and meetings. I jotted a series of notes in the diary, each one representing a different day on the road:

> ...The gas line plugged and we chugged into an all-night garage where we waited and waited and waited.
> ...Sick relatives had called for us and we were stuck along the road.
> ...Two blown-out tires and one flat at same time.
> ...A dead engine to be replaced.
> ...Replaced carburetor for $50. *(The diary)*

My blathering about this garbage can of trash closely resembled the sound emanating from under the hood. Art admonished me not to say anything more about the Renault, but rather to have faith for it. I closed my mouth and allowed God to have the last word. Driving home from helping a relative in Tacoma, my husband swerved to miss a pedestrian and hit a row of mailboxes and a sign. The hood and grill were crumpled and the lights destroyed. We towed home the battered remains and pushed them under the carport. There the Renault sat—except for the unnerving number of occasions we pulled it out, jury-rigged it, and entreated it to take us to where we were headed and back to the carport...all before dark!

Our sons, David and Mert, attempted to revive a '49 Dodge we had diagnosed as lifeless long before. Those two *mechanically adept* sons tried to install a replacement engine in the Dodge, only to discover they had the wrong one. They repeated the operation and the second replacement didn't function. Then they read the manual. Aha! They should have taken off the transmission first. Subsequent to that repair, the oil leaked out and a mechanic discovered the boys had installed a gasket incorrectly. Next a racket—sounding like a doomed-for-slaughter chicken—grew with each mile, until a flare-up under the hood sent flames in the air. We never knew the cause, but by then we'd come to appreciate the phrase, "Have you read the manual?"

Bless our agent at Safeco Insurance. She'd assigned us a comprehensive plan which included fire coverage. On the next outing, the Dodge with a replaced motor, repairs after fire damage, and 200,000 miles couldn't climb the hill in Addy. *Self*—that's my preferred pronoun—carrying more than a million miles on her feet, had to get out and push. Thankfully, the results paid dividends. We arrived at the parsonage of Pastor Pete who'd asked to meet us. His brother Jim, cigarette in mouth, met us at the door, and within minutes disclosed that his entire being was bound by addiction. Arthur recounted his own liberation from cigarettes half a century earlier, and Jim, in tears, asked for laying on of hands. He looked up, his face glowing, "I felt that spirit come out of me. I know I have been liberated."

Arthur counseled Jim to remain alert and to walk closely with the Lord. Otherwise, he could become vulnerable to a new attack. The preacher said to Arthur, "I have been failing in my faith and needing a pastor of my own. Thank you."

From there we visited one of our grandsons. He told of a soreness in his mouth the doctor called pyorrhea—another name for periodontitis which usually requires treatment to save the teeth. Arthur prayed for his healing and said, "I don't know if this applies, but I wonder if there has been criticism or wrong attitudes about Christians."

"Yes," the boy replied. "I must make something right." Which he did…that same day.

We limped on home and bequeathed the Dodge to Ron Guderian to restore and use for his commute to the University of Washington and to haul around a Sunday school class of high school boys from Emmanuel Bible Church. The next time we saw the Dodge, it had been artistically embellished by those boys to look like a hippie wagon.

In 1967, not long after Arthur gave up on the Renault and the '49 Dodge, he awakened to strikes of lightning through his chest. Issues with his heart were not new, but this attack was so incapacitating he could barely breathe. Weak and immobile, he lay prostrated, petitioning for strength even to sit up. God didn't answer with a divine miracle as Arthur expected, and the slightest exertion or stress flattened him for hours.

Managing Arthur's 24-hour care left me no time and energy to parent Edward and Stacey. I asked Welfare to look for new accommodations. In November 1967, Stacey went to another family, and in January 1968, we took Edward to the Vancouver Boys Academy. My spirit tore within me as I saw their grim, forlorn faces. But I realized we'd made a temporary home for these youngsters and had to trust God to guard over them.

The silence at our place was unprecedented. Only Janice, not yet 16, remained. She was in school all day, so for the first time in five decades I could hear the walls creaking, the fridge humming, and the clock in the corner ticking. Arthur and I sat in our chairs for hours reading the Bible—until he fell asleep with God's Words on his lips, or his mouth open in prayer. After a couple of months of this spiritual therapy, Arthur said, "I hear the crickets in my shoes chirping to hop again. It's time to call on folks."

I was about to say he had no reliable wheels nor the fortitude to fiddle with junkers, when he decreed, "We are going to get a new— a genuinely new—car."

We visited the dealer in Port Angeles and purchased a yellow Dodge Coronet. Arthur assured me that driving placed no strain on his recovering heart. "I will not be walking from town to town like Paul and the apostles," he said, "nor suffering in blistering desert heat next to a lame chariot."

Arthur drove that car north to Alaska, south to Nevada, east to North Dakota, and west to Neah Bay…wherever God sent him. Liberation! Emancipation! Rejuvenation! He'd get in that spiffy sedan and go—150,000 miles in three years—the record of which is documented in another chapter.

By the time I was free to travel long distances with Arthur, the Coronet had passed those 150,000 miles and become a bag of loose screws and bolts. Its last hurrah took us in June 1972, to a Corey reunion in Oregon hosted by Arthur's sister Ruth and her husband Harry Bruck. I thought breakdowns might delay our arrival and save me from the replay of my worry-wart nightmare, where I'd be wearing an unsuitable outfit and shuffling from foot to foot, finding nowhere to stand and nothing to say. Instead, the car performed its duty and we were welcomed into the crowd of sixty relatives. Stories were told and memories embellished.

Ruth couldn't resist telling one on Arthur. "Remember?" she asked, "when you visited us on the island and I made clam chowder for lunch?"

Arthur smirked, which freed Ruth to tease. "I watched as you fastidiously searched for each morsel you thought was seafood."

She paused and glanced at those who were listening. "But I had not yet put in the clams you didn't like. You picked out the bacon."

The story was not new, but equally hilarious as ever. I turned to Arthur, "And you threw away the bacon. Your favorite meat!"

In attendance were Arthur's sister and brother-in-law, Hazel and Emil Bruck, about whom I have already written, as well as his sister Esther. Esther's first husband had died while very young, and Arthur had often assisted her with projects and repairs. Later, Esther remarried and we continued our visits, becoming close friends with her new family, including stepdaughter, LaVerne, and her husband, Paul Nielsen. At the party, we also caught up with Harold and Vera and Albert and Hilda—two brothers and wives closest to us in age.

Dozens of relatives from later generations were present, but missing on the occasion were Arthur's brothers, Jim, who didn't travel much, and Lester, who had passed away. For years, Arthur had been concerned for the salvation of these two older brothers. In 1969, he had gone to visit Lester at his Ketners Point place on Fox Island. Lester welcomed us and our brief message from God. Leaving the island, Arthur prayed that the Spirit of God would squeeze the Word through the cracks of his resistance. Not long after our visit, Lester died. Will we see him in heaven? I trust so.

The absence of two at the reunion was the harbinger of numbered days for all of us. However, *beyond* numbering were the days of the Dodge Coronet. Its end ushered in another revolutionary concept of Corey cars—exchange the used for new every year or so. To Arthur, new cars were badges of God's blessing. But to me they added an apprehension: *How would relatives and friends receive us in lorries, newer and loftier than their own?*

--TWELVE--

Lofty lorries and loved ones

In 1972, after the demise of the Coronet, we became the owners of a new Ford Grand Torino Station Wagon. I would have eliminated the luxury—this Ford touted power steering, power brakes, heavy duty shocks, power windows, and wide tires. Arthur added a plaque—**THE KING IS COMING**.

Grand Torino with THE KING IS COMING, 1972

On our first drive, while we waited for a ferry, a woman came to the door, "You must be Christians."

The fancy car had not caught her attention. Instead, the words of the sign had invited her to knock on our window. The woman told us that she was torn apart by obsessive thoughts and irrational terror, and that she had lost all hope for peace. That day, before the ferry loaded, we led her to faith and victory.

We crossed Puget Sound on the ferry to join 75 relatives in a surprise 50th anniversary celebration of Arthur's brother Harold and his wife Vera, hosted by their son Dick and his wife Ann. En route, I asked Arthur to park our high style limousine out of eyesight. Instead, he parked right in front and strutted as proud and tall as his five feet, nine and one quarter inches would allow. Not a soul even mentioned our mode of arrival. After that we accompanied Harold and Vera to the 50th reunion of our Tacoma Lincoln High School class. None of those old timers, most of whom we had last seen in the early twenties, cared a hoot about what we were driving. They were much more interested in knowing where we'd been and what we'd done. Arthur was in his element—hours' worth of interaction with all those former classmates and his brother and Vera. Even I was engaged, conceding to Arthur I was glad he'd snubbed my niggling about feeling out of place and out of style, and had insisted we go. I became doubly grateful for the camaraderie, when—a mere half year later in January 1974—Harold passed away. Six months following Harold's death, his son Dick died in an aviation accident. Those events with Arthur's brother and his family will remain in our hearts until we join them for eternity.

By the end of 1974, Arthur negotiated at Anderson Ford for a less than lofty limo, one with better economy and requiring the newest thing—unleaded gas. The shopping-cart-sized Ford promptly took us to see my sister Eleanor and her husband in California. Howard was ill with cancer and the effects of chemotherapy. Although he didn't respond to any discussion of the spiritual or eternal, we assured him of God's love. When Howard died in 1976, Eleanor wrote me that she was praying out loud when she sensed he was in his last moments, and she was content that he seemed at peace.

After my sister cleared up the paperwork, she came to visit us for several weeks. She and I gabbed long into the night, only moving to refill our coffee cups. We picked up the next morning where we had left off, sounding to Arthur like the henhouse after the first round of eggs was laid. Ever since my wedding and subsequent childbearing years, my little sister and I had never experienced such an uninterrupted conversation.

The Ford took us to Tacoma where we retraced our childhood. First, we dined in the Stanley and Seafort's Restaurant at 115 E. 34th, the exact address of our growing-up residence. We used the new bathrooms facing the solid wood stairs I remembered from the epoch of our youth. The shape of the east side of the building, which jutted out over the backyard, hadn't changed. The diner also encompassed the home of Uncle Charlie Elmer, Aunt Mabel, and Cousins Bernice, Mildred, and Charles. A blacktop parking lot spread across the site that had been the dwelling of Uncle Joe, Aunt Ida, and Cousins Lois and George. My sister and I stood at the restaurant window and looked over the bay below. We chatted about the outings to Mount Rainier and the picnics at Brown's Point. Eleanor laughed, "Did we ever have a happy childhood, growing up with aunts, uncles, and cousins on our own vantage point highland."

We reminisced about our cousins. George had been the first to die. "Such a difficult experience," Eleanor said, referring to the surgery to his spine that left him paralyzed and suffering from severe pain.

I added, "Art and I visited him at the University of Washington Hospital on several occasions. For two years he was in and out of multiple surgeries while they experimented to find a remedy for his damaged nerves. No medical treatment alleviated his misery or gave him prospect of recovery."

My voice cracked as I spoke of those visits. "Art prayed for George's healing and for God to wash him with peace. Not long after, George died in his hospital room—a mercy, though a sorrowful time for his youthful family."

We recalled that during the same season of 1962, Ruth, our cousin Charles' wife of 18 years, died of cancer. My sister said, "She was such a sweetheart, and what a talent for singing! I remember how she was always dressed *to the nines*—made me feel like a country bumpkin."

I agreed, "When she sent me a nearly new outfit, it was stylish and attractive. I felt halfway put together, no matter how cash strapped we were. I have such fond memories of Charles, so fun-loving and adventurous...though lots younger than you and I."

"Only you, not I," Eleanor chuckled. "He and I were mere pipsqueaks when you disappeared from the Tacoma scene."

Eleanor asked about Lillian whom Charles had married in 1969, and I updated her on their happy home where we'd occasionally stayed.

My sister and I talked about our cousin Bernice and her husband Edgar Hetrick, who had recently returned to Washington State from Hawaii. We spoke of our cousin Mildred Hunter, a talented pianist who, like I, got her musical start with Naoma. "Did you know?" I remarked, "She's in her eighties and still plays piano at the First Presbyterian Church."

Our table was ready and we continued the conversation all through lunch with Arthur joining in. Afterwards, he drove us to the cemetery where our father had been laid to rest. We motored by the house where Arthur grew up. We checked in with our cousin Lois (Uncle Joe's daughter) and her husband Ernie Radomske at an information booth located in the depot where our father had handled baggage for the trains. Lois, between the ages of Eleanor and me, had served as a physical therapist in the US Army during World War II, and we had been proud of her striking professional appearance and her accomplishments. Like so many kin who hadn't initially understood Arthur's persuasion, she and her husband had become one with us in spirit. Before we left the train station, Lois and Ernie arranged to visit us.

As Eleanor and I hugged goodbye, our eyes spilled over and we each searched in our purses for Kleenex. I told my sister, "Wouldn't it be wonderful if you could come to live on our property? Be near all of us who love you?"

Eleanor blew her nose and shook her head. I knew the answer without awaiting her response. My sister had promised to assist Kay, her invalid sister-in-law, until death separated them. At this writing more than ten years later, Eleanor is living in Kay's house where she stays 24 hours, 7 days a week. Kay will not allow anyone else entrance and refuses to move into a convalescent center. We are saddened there seems no end to this burden that is taking a toll on my sister's health and strength. May God repay her for the sacrifice! I know He will, for she is my precious sister and His beloved child.[19]

Back in our own neighborhood, in December 1976 we took several trips in the Ford to move our daughter Janice and her four-year-old son, Tony, into the home of Bob and Ruth Richardson (Bill Richardson's parents) while they were on vacation. Janice's marriage had ended, and this tranquil place of recovery was next door to Bill and Elizabeth. But not all was tranquil. Janice had barely settled in when she phoned one morning. "The house almost burned down last night. But we're okay. Thank the Lord!"

"What happened?" I gasped.

"I was sleeping soundly—better than in years—with the window open and the creek gurgling." She said. "Suddenly, I was startled awake. I hurried to Tony's room and opened the door to a cloud of smoke. His pillow had dropped onto the heater and was smoldering. I grabbed him in a blanket, sat him outside, and went back to get the pillow which I tossed out into the rain."

I interrupted, "God awakened you."

She went on, "That's not all. The second fire was worse than the first."

"What do you mean, second fire?"

"We aired the house, thanked the Lord for saving us and went back to bed. When I was awakened again, the front door was ablaze. Flames were so close to Ruth's closet full of winter coats, I thought they'd burn up. Tony was my bigger concern, so I rushed him out the other door and phoned Liz and Bill. They arrived with hoses and buckets, and put out the fire."

Janice caught her breath and I started to ask a question about the damage. She kept talking. "Bill said the pillow had ignited the fir needles under the gravel and flames had crept along the ground. But he assured me, 'Don't worry, Janice. All that matters is you are both safe.'"

Arthur and I were concerned that the owners would be upset. Not so. Bob Richardson likewise spoke of gratitude to God that no one was hurt, "The porch and steps can be repaired, and we have insurance for that."

Soon after Janice and Tony were resettled, Arthur and I drove three hours to Bellevue, near Seattle, to visit our next-to-youngest daughter Marian and her husband Don. As we traveled, I flashed back to Marian's bumpy ride since high school. Afflicted by one infirmity after another, she had changed schools, switched jobs, and moved from place to place. As her contacts and choices led her away from God, and she floundered without a sense of direction, all we could do was wait on the Father whose love for her dwarfed any of our human sentiments. Marian moved to California where she became entangled with Don—a self-proclaimed atheist. Arthur and I were nearly overcome in sorrow when they were married, yet our hearts were open to them both, trusting God would bring Don to repentance and faith. When the couple moved to Bellevue, we thought God was preparing a way. Nonetheless, during this visit at the end of 1976, a barrier remained. Don avoided us, and we perceived Marian had chosen his party-centered lifestyle for herself.

One week later, Marian phoned, "Mom, I'm calling to tell you I have made things right with God. I told Him I have messed up and am so sorry. I want to apologize to you and Dad for what I've put you through. These past years I have wandered far from what you taught and lived. Each choice I made added to the distance away from the presence of God. I never wanted to be caught in a relationship that was wrong, but I couldn't drag myself from Don who made me feel special and accepted, and who gave me a good time—at least what I thought was a good time."

Marian caught her breath in a sob, while I sputtered from my own lumpy throat, "Thank you, Lord Jesus!"

She went on, "What I know today is that God has forgiven me, and I believe you and Dad will forgive me. Because that's who you are. All these years you have prayed and committed, followed and pursued. You have not condemned. Instead you have trusted God, although I couldn't."

I opened my mouth, but no words came. Marian finished, "Please pray for me. I don't know how to live as a witness when my yearning to please the Lord is in conflict with what Don expects of me. I don't know how to submit to him and walk with the Lord."

I wiped my face on the corner of my apron. "Dad and I will intercede, and God will show you the way."

After Marian hung up, I found Arthur and together we petitioned God to enfold her in His arms and to give her His wisdom. "And Lord Jesus," Arthur added, "manifest your power in Don's life so he will turn to you."

Marian kept her oath to God and lived in accountability to Him while seeking to hold her marriage together. Don didn't find the Lord; instead, he pursued other women and intensified his ridicule of Marian and her faith. When she remained steadfast and composed, he filed for divorce.

It wasn't the way we anticipated God would speak into their lives, but He knew the end from the beginning. As the Bible says in Jeremiah 29:11: HE KNEW THE PLANS HE HAD FOR (HER), PLANS TO PROSPER AND NOT HARM, PLANS TO GIVE HER HOPE AND A FUTURE. We'd wait and see what His plans were. Two years later, in 1980,

Marian married Dennis Alwine, a believer who loves her and their children without reservation.

Arthur replaced the small Ford with a Dodge Aspen. Connected to the Aspen is an interaction at a restaurant in Tacoma. "I know you," said a young man, "On Whidbey Island, you prayed for me to find a godly wife. And here she is."

We celebrated with enthusiasm, right there in the restaurant where other patrons could hear the story of God's involvement. "Now," the young man said, "Would you ask God to bless our home?"

The Aspen was the first of our autos to have a CB radio installed. Citizen Band short distance frequencies allow common folks to transmit and receive messages—though the screeching, rattling, and popping noise didn't sound in my ears like messaging. Arthur said he would get the permit and I would have to practice operating the buttons and microphone while he drove. *No thank you very much!*

In 1978, we traded up for a Buick. I suggested Arthur could let the CB radio go with the Aspen, but no. What a racket the machine made and what a bother. We never succeeded in broadcasting the gospel of Jesus by CB to other drivers on the road. Be as it may, Arthur persisted in putting the CB radio in his new cars, emphasizing that the airwaves were a creative way to preach. "Perhaps," I countered, "such evangelism might be possible if I could drive while you preach and manage the technology."

I didn't know the reason for a new vehicle in 1979, but we turned in the old for new once again. I was so *un*impressed, I didn't bother to record the model nor give her a name. Arthur was quick to take this unidentified set of wheels to his associates for dedication, not to me—I was having an attitude. Dedicated service this car provided—in spite of my opposition! At the first meeting we attended in no-name machine, Mr. Thomas came forward to confess he was an alcoholic. His sincerity of repentance and his request for release from bondage inspired seven godly men to surround him. I was amazed to see the victory in his visage and the rejoicing in the congregation. Next, a young woman told of a growth in her breast. Two hours later at the after-meeting, she testified the bulge had disappeared. A couple thanked God for the restoration of their marriage. They explained, "Two years ago we had been on the verge of splitting up when Brother Corey prayed. Now we are like newlyweds."

Hmm—spiritual results enabled by the car about which I'd stewed! Yet, I had plenty of reason to dislike No-Name. She had a propensity to stall at inopportune locations or to ignore the driver's orders. On one occasion, she anchored her wheels and balked at climbing a steep road. Arthur weaseled her backwards onto a narrow road with cliffs on both sides. We were stalled and stuck. My pushing power was equal to a bird, so my husband held onto the steering wheel and shoved too. Eventually we two near-octogenarians scrimmaged the carriage out of the way in time for a loaded grain truck to barrel by! With urgency to heaven and a reprimand to the nameless machine, Arthur managed to coax her backwards up that steep hill—I can't guess how far—and leave her at a repair shop.

Time for a replacement—we were in sync this time. No-Name was traded up for a new Ford. To give the Ford a comfort test, we took a vacation to visit John and Virginia McLennan in their new ministry at Christ for the Nations in Dallas, Texas. The atmosphere was warm, and we were blessed to see our oldest daughter and her husband in a fulfilling teaching ministry.

We continued to the Midwest to visit my brother, Herbert, and his wife, Edith, whom we had seen several times after they moved back to the USA from mission work in Cuba. Their love for the Lord was strong and we were refreshed. Later that year, they returned the favor and came on Amtrak with their sons, Roger and Richard, to visit us. We celebrated with sightseeing and reminiscing and eating and laughing, and I'm glad we did—for we never saw Herbert again before he passed away in 1985.

Back to the upgrade of cars. This time to a fancier Ford—a comfortable, semi-luxury LTD. I'd barely filled the pockets and glove box with Kleenex, wipes, maps, nail files, hand cream, and other essentials, when I discovered Arthur cleaning with uncharacteristic zeal. I ventured, "You're not thinking to get rid of this one, are you?"

He didn't answer, so I added, "I like this comfy coach. Can't we keep it a little longer?"

No discussion. Instead he conscripted our daughter Marian. Two hours later, Arthur returned in a Mazda, and Marian came behind in the Ford LTD. I had decided to say nothing if Arthur drove home in a new conveyance. Instead, I stewed under my breath, *No trade in of the old for the new? We now have two cars?* Too hard to keep quiet on the subject, so I wrote down:

> I fail to see the usefulness of two cars when I can't even drive one of them. Henceforth, I glue my tongue to the palate of my mouth! *(The diary)*

In April 1986, Arthur turned in the Mazda and bought a Mercury Marquis. He delivered the Ford LTD to Bob Richardson who promptly loaned it to one of our missionary families for their deputation. I chose to ignore Arthur's I-told-you-so grin designed to validate the wisdom of having kept that second set of wheels. Nonetheless, I couldn't dispel my point of view about these new transports, and I shut my mouth when we arrived in elegant style at the households of friends who drove clunkers. But I was done grumbling on this subject.

God had chosen to deliver beyond all we could ask or think, and I could and *would* choose to be grateful. In embracing gratitude as an attitude, my focus shifted to the sideline benefits I received because of Art's penchant for reliable roadsters.

The Mercury Marquis, 1986

--THIRTEEN--

Gratitude is an attitude

To illustrate those secondary benefits, I've backed up to an earlier time—1968, the Year of the Yellow Dodge Coronet. After Arthur had tested the Coronet on a few quests, he happily tucked me into the shotgun seat as often as I felt a need to go—in particular to call on distressed relatives. He took me to Tacoma to the home of my Uncle Elmer and Aunt Edna—to run their errands, take them to medical appointments, and scrub their bathroom. We used those visits to explain the Word and to ask God to give them understanding. *Oh magnify the Lord!* After half a century of hearing our witness, these loved ones assured us—albeit wearing the shadow of eternity on their faces—they were ready to be received by Jesus.

At the same time, my cousin Naoma was beginning to fade. The Dodge made possible our trips to help her—for she had no one else who loved her like we did. Through all our years apart, each week she had written me and expected in return a full disclosure of all that went on around here. A self-supporting business woman, Naoma initially couldn't comprehend the way we lived—dependent on folks who were moved to give. But I never doubted her love for us or her love for the Lord. Naoma also had a legendary affinity for her cats, and prayed for them as earnestly as I prayed for her. Once she wrote me how God had answered her prayer and put Susie the cat to sleep before the vet had to come and do it.

We settled Naoma into a nursing facility, settled legal matters, cleaned out her hoard of stuff—taking loads to Goodwill and the dump. Her bungalow was worth tuppence, but at least helped cover her costs in the facility. Naoma bemoaned the lack of resources to bequeath us. "Pshaw," I said, "You have meant more to us than all the resources in the world."

We loaded up heirloom furniture with the fruit carvings on the panels and drawer handles, handmade quilts of traditional designs, and a scenic picture covered by vintage wavy glass and framed in blackened oak. David and Vi took the ebony finished piano used for my childhood lessons.[20] We lugged crates full of letters—including all that I had ever written her. In the stash I found a 1937 letter in which I had responded to her questions about our ministry. Reading these words floated me back to the emotion I'd felt:

> Art has never made any drastic move unless I was perfectly willing, and truly he never urged or argued or forced me into it. I know the Lord has called him for full time service...I haven't a single doubt but that all we need will be supplied, and the most wonderful thing about it is we have never had to ask for anything, except to ask the Lord...
>
> About Arthur and a job—if you were to follow him around for say about a week you would see that he couldn't hold a regular job as many have suggested. I hope you can feel that all is well—and there is surely one thing you can do. Pray for us—that the Lord will use us in His own way and that we will know His mind. Lots and lots and lots of love from ME.
>
> Your loving cousin, Marg[21]

By the spring of 1968, following the deaths of Uncle Elmer, Aunt Edna, and Cousin Naoma, Arthur was gearing up for a long mission to the Midwest with me at his side. I was uneasy to leave responsibilities unattended, but instead of whining at Arthur, I focused on sharing my hesitations with God. The Heavenly Father saw my concern and knew my thoughts! Two days before the travel date, we received notice that Eleanor's and Ron's baby Jeffrey had been born—one month early. Arthur allowed, "The timing was orchestrated by God. You are free to stay."

Before Arthur headed east into the sunrise he dropped me in the Ballard district of Seattle to attend to the mother and baby—even to assist Ron in shopping for essentials. After a week, I was able to go home to my mother and daughter who depended on me, and my husband could continue farther in the opposite direction.

During my husband's absence of two long months, he sent me letters and kept a detailed journal from which I have picked excerpts of interest:

> While driving in Montana, my error was reading a sign wrong—my eyes had captured 5 miles instead of .5 miles—but surely by God's preplanning, as it allowed me to visit the Stewart family, supporters of Phil and Darlene.
>
> Next leg of the trip, I went in a 50-mile out-of-the-way circle, which opened opportunity at a truck stop cafe with a driver ripe for counsel, before I made it to my planned stop at Harry and Ella Guderians' farm in Thornhill, Manitoba. In the midst of May snow and wind and more snow, the Guderians took me to Winkler for a new wool suit. Best one I ever had. Guess so! Cost about $100. I was as well attired as any man at the Mennonite Brethren Church where I preached that Sunday.
>
> I stopped in Wisconsin where I was taken to see James, a deaf man. He told me he had accepted the Lord and asked to be baptized, but his minister said

baptism was pointless, even erroneous. I opened to the scriptures on baptism and spoke slowly—mouthing the words so he could read my lips. "Well then," James said. "Let me be baptized right now."

The outcome was a baptismal service for many believers in the river next to the church that was promoting the false teaching. What a victory for the truth! ...Much love, Arthur

Two months was a test for Arthur too. After God freed him up, he drove 900 miles without rest…other than catnaps beside the road. I asked, "Why did you drive so long, and arrive so worn out?"

He said, "I had to get home to you!"

During the following season our responsibilities changed. My mother, Edith Phenicie, passed away in her sleep in August 25, 1969, and my youngest daughter graduated from high school. Arthur felt freer to say he sensed me alongside him when he received the call to go, and I felt less free to say I couldn't.

We were headed east, intending to go as far as Spokane. Car trouble stopped us at Wenatchee. Arthur pulled out the address of Darrell Morrison, son of our friends, Oakland and India. We had no way to phone ahead, so just showed up. *Such a time I have with that…just showing up.* After welcoming us, Darrell unloaded spiritual and emotional burdens he was carrying, proclaiming more than once, "God knew I needed to talk with you. He sent you, and I thank Him."

As we prepared to leave, Darrell walked us to the parking lot. He suggested, almost as an afterthought, "Let me know if there is anything I can do to help you. Maybe dental care?"

Arthur responded, "Yes, there is. My wife is having problems with her teeth."

Darrell grinned, "Well, that's something I can fix. Next time you're in town, come to my clinic during office hours."

Which we did! Darrell had a cancellation at the precise moment we arrived, so he spent three hours on my teeth. After he finished, he set up another appointment to include an afternoon in the dental chair, overnight accommodations, and a morning follow-up. Arthur queried the cost, and Darrell answered, "I knew you'd ask that. Let's pray about it. You pray and I pray, and the Lord will lead."

Darrell took permanent care of the teeth that hurt—pulled them all. He prepared me a full set of dentures, and assured us the cost was covered by Art's counsel from the Lord. No longer did I have a mish mash of bad teeth. Though, I might mention a downside: Wearing a mouthful of new, white, false teeth, I had to learn how to eat and speak all over again. In the following years, whenever Arthur or I had a dental concern or required a new set of dentures, Darrell donated skill and resources. Concurrently, Darrell and his wife Jan were growing in the Lord. They became part of our team and organized meetings to coincide with our visits—for dentistry or not—and invited many colleagues and neighbors.

While I was choosing an attitude of gratitude, God was seeing my needs and meeting them—dentistry was only one. All I had to do was trust and obey—as the song says:

> When we walk with the Lord in the light of His Word,
> What a glory He sheds on our way!
> While we do His good will, He abides with us still,
> And with all who will trust and obey.[22]

--FOURTEEN--

The majesty of creation

God has supplied every necessity for our journeys. But He has also given us beauty along the way. Our travels for the kingdom have opened our eyes to a splendor, majesty, and glory that never failed to spark in us a burst of worship toward the Creator. To begin this theme, I've backed up to 1965 to include Arthur's log following our trip through the Southwest in David's Rambler:

> I am overwhelmed by the splendid sights of the Grand Canyon. HOW THE FIRMAMENT SHOWETH HIS HANDIWORK...AND DAY UNTO DAY UTTERETH SPEECH. I felt we should uncover our heads and take off our shoes at such manifestation of His wondrous works. I observe that many are awed and humbled, but to others it's nothing more than sightseeing. We traversed the painted desert of the Navajo Indians and were enveloped in an unusual beauty of light and color and sparkle and shadow. (*Arthur Corey*)

While on this safari through the desert, we stopped at a new Bible Church among the widely scattered hogans—the pole, bark, and mud dwellings of the Navajo. We met a missionary and his wife and two high school sons. What a difficult field and so little fruit for the effort. Yet God loves the native Navajo peoples. May God bless His servants who are laboring under such disheartening circumstances!

In 1968, Arthur wrote me from Alaska. He'd driven the yellow Dodge Coronet to meet up with our son Merton and his friend David Wilder who had flown there in a small plane. Although Art painted for me the awesome scenery and grandeur, he seemed more verbose in describing his intimidation in flying over it:

> People tell me planes are the way to get around in Alaska, and I accepted the invitation to ride in a small aircraft. Uneasy, to say the least, I took off my hat and remarked: "A MAN WHO PRAYS WITH HIS HEAD COVERED DISHONORS HIS HEAD."
> They laughed at my seeming temerity. I was truthful though, and during the flight I continually rehearsed the verse I had read on the way to the airport: I SHALL NOT DIE BUT LIVE AND DECLARE THE WORKS OF THE LORD. We traversed the peaks and glaciers, riding so high in that puny manmade machine and so at the mercy of the powers that be...and the wind and down drafts, and the shakes and bumps. I had trouble enjoying the scenery while reminding the Lord I still expected to declare His works...Love to you, Arthur

Arthur filled one page with details about helping Ray Johnson get married and taking Mert to buy new shoes. And he was sure I wouldn't approve of his correcting female attendants for making remarks about the beards on the attending men.

He told of visiting Bill Richardson's brother and sister-in-law, George and Judy, in Cantwell and eating meals in which every possible food was garnished by wild blueberries. (I think he emphasized this because he knows I've never been a fan of blueberries).

In his log, Art portrayed more from God's easel of beauty and the lessons he learned along the road:

> Toward Whitehorse, I drove into the most beautiful rainbow I'd ever seen—stretched clear across a lake with each end on a shore. A full, brilliant circle, like entering a gorgeous portal. I was so entranced by the beauty, I didn't stop for a couple of hitchhikers. Immediately, I heard the Lord's voice in my conscience. I tried to justify my actions—reminding God how the Royal Canadian Mounted Police had stopped me to ask if I'd seen hitchhikers dressed in such and such...which I had. The two had stolen a pickup they later ditched. God countered my rationale with: GIVE TO HIM THAT ASKETH OF THEE. Following this conversation with the Lord, sure enough, ahead were two others seeking a ride.[23] (*Arthur Corey*)

Art drove with the boys for two days. After leaving them at one of their homes, he continued south and east toward Three Hills, Alberta, where he was scheduled to meet up again with our son and his friend David. I share another installment of Art's story:

> About 30 miles from the home where I left the hitchhiking boys, I felt a rattling and grinding and banging as if universal joints had given out. A sports sedan pulled ahead and the driver signaled me to stop and take care of a bad tire. I thanked the man and thanked the Lord for nudging him. When I stopped at Grande Prairie to replace the disintegrated tire, the guy was waiting. "I want to hear more," he said, "from this traveling preacher who speaks to God as if He is standing on the same soil."
>
> I was in a Spirit-electrified element, thanks to a divine delay I'd thought inconvenient. (*Arthur Corey*)

Arthur called me the first day of September from Three Hills. He had been invited to preach in the Big Tabernacle of Prairie Bible Institute where so many of our children had studied. My husband said he was missing me, and I said the feeling was mutual. He followed with, "You are to get a flight to Great Falls and meet me there."

I said, "I can't swallow the cost and deal with the difficulty of getting to the airport."

He argued, "I just want you to have an exciting adventure."

Me and my big mouth! I had said to him I was thinking of doing something fun since he'd been gone so long. He, apparently, didn't want to miss out.

The following day, Dave Wilder and Merton returned to Joyce from their aeronautic enterprise in Alaska. What a relief. Then Arthur called, confirming his expectation I would take the flight. Two days later, I landed in Great Falls, and indeed both of us were glad to be together. Everything was back to normal—we missed our first turn and drove the wrong direction out of the airport.

One of the stops we made was in Helena, MT, to see Onolee Wetherald. We hadn't spoken to Onolee in more than 20 years. Seeing her stirred to memory the closeness we'd had with the Wetherald clan in the '30s and '40s. Onolee's sister, Joy Belle, had lived for months with us in the grange house and been like an older sister to our girls. Joy's efficient, loving attention to the children had allowed me to minister with Arthur in the community. In fact, Joy, at 16 years, had saved Marilyn's life by pressing a wad of flour into a hand wound where a scissor blade had severed an artery.[24]

After hugging Onolee goodbye, Arthur and I took our fun adventure to Yellowstone National Park. We spent the day marveling at the artistic phenomena of our God—the erupting geysers, the bubbling pools, and the bizarre landscape. We followed signs to the Lewis and Clark Caverns, where a lift carried us up a steep cliff that left me reeling from the height. We visited red and rocky regions and toured Hoover Dam. The scenes I saw with Arthur were beyond my wildest dreams, though—upon returning home—I realized none could surpass the beautiful waterways of Puget Sound and the Straits of Juan de Fuca, nestled between the Olympics and the Cascades.

To this day, it's impossible for me to comprehend how earthlings choose to believe all these spectacles occurred by happenstance or big bang or billions of years of evolution—or how unbelievers can avoid or deny the voice of their Creator whose plan from the start was for them to see Him in creation and seek to know Him.

Mount Rainier, 1937

--FIFTEEN--

Take the wings of the morning

Travel genes flowed through Arthur's blood, not for sightseeing—as rewarding as that was—but for serving. In 1971, as requests came for another trip to the Dominican Republic (DR), his spirit began repeating the verse from Psalm 139:9: IF I TAKE THE WINGS OF THE MORNING AND DWELL IN THE UTTERMOST PARTS OF THE SEA; EVEN THERE SHALL THY HAND LEAD ME, AND THY RIGHT HAND SHALL HOLD ME. Back in '66, we'd gone to visit Marilyn and Allen. This second trip would be to assist Phil and Darlene, their two children, Mark (10) and Melanie (7), and the premature Dominican infant they were adopting. Before leaving on the first trip, God had dealt with my unwillingness to leave behind those for whom I was responsible to go to a land rattled by unrest. For this safari, I was quick to pack my bags. The DR had settled its internal hostilities, and we were virtually empty nesters who could help those fledglings who'd landed far from our nestage.

On the way across the continent we experienced the usual delays for car repairs. However, other diversions were less disheartening. Arthur left his glasses and 58-cent hat in Harry Guderian's car and we had to reverse direction to rendezvous with him. In rural

Minnesota, the odometer read 128282.8 so we had to stop by the road and look at it for a spell before going on to Minneapolis. One morning, Arthur told me to stay in bed in a *not-so-nice* hotel, while he went out to get me coffee, which arrived cold. We got lost in the Smokey Mountains, and I swallowed one of my new teeth…to name a few distractions.

In Miami, Allen and Marilyn, by this time serving at West Indies Mission headquarters, took us to the airport. Phil and Darlene rescued us at customs on the DR side, where we were trying to explain (without common language) the use of an adding machine. Our first impressions of the country were the changes. Low cost apartments had replaced the shacks along a much-improved highway. The streets were quiet, other than the beeping of horns and the happy sounds of children and dogs. And the scenery refreshed my spirit.

Tropical Landscape in the Dominican Republic, 1971

I dug into household projects, mainly caring for Mark and Melanie and preparing meals. Ingredients with Spanish names required translation, but I'd had practice on the previous trip. My biggest concern was for Darlene, so thin and tired, and so intently focused on the 3lb 12oz infant the pediatrician said could die as easily as a butterfly. Flooding my thought was the notion, *Darlene isn't going to have milk to nurse this baby if she doesn't eat better and get more sleep.* Oops, I'd forgotten for a moment this caramel-toned baby was actually adopted, and the new mother had no option of mother's milk.

Arthur, too, was burdened for the little one. One day after communing with God in the room set aside as isolation for Darlene and the baby, he said, "I have never felt the presence of the angel of the Lord as strongly as I have today in this room. Tiny Tim will be okay."

Basking in that benediction of the Spirit, Arthur was primed for reaching out. These are his recorded words:

> My first message was about Naaman's healing...but where would I have been without the translation by Brother Samuels?! Studies of Spanish took up much time during the week. I was revitalized when a group of young people said I was *muy inteligente* (very intelligent) and would learn the language if I stayed three or four months. Such flattery was quite inspirational. *(Arthur Corey)*

Arthur also reported on a thrilling service that took place on the roof of one home. Talk about multicultural. There were Haitians, Dominicans, Canadians, Jamaicans, and Americans. This scenario reminded him of the grand celebration promised in Revelation 7:9: A MULTITUDE WHICH NO MAN CAN NUMBER WILL BE ASSEMBLED OUT OF EVERY TONGUE AND TRIBE AND KINDRED AND NATION AND PEOPLE.

At another service in which Arthur spoke, several in attendance received the Lord into their lives. In describing the meeting, he said, "I spoke for an hour and ten minutes, using much scripture."

Phil countered with, "TOO MUCH scripture."

To which Arthur replied, "I don't think so, as no one else remonstrated. What a change from congregations at home, where at 20 minutes people begin to check watches."

As we prepared to leave for home, Arthur and I were again *sick and afflicted.* The digestive malady hung on for the duration of the trip home—first a fidgety flight to Miami, then an episodic road trip with broken speed laws to get to rest stops—sometimes one with the door locked, or one with a single room for men and women and no toilet paper. It was a toss-up as to which was worse, the unkempt facilities or a field on the prairies with nowhere to hide. In one such situation, I told Arthur I would gladly use an outhouse and a Sears catalog as we did during the middle decades of the century.

We were delayed at the Arizona state line while agents confiscated cotton I had picked a week earlier at a southern plantation, causing us to arrive late at the home of Art's sister Esther in California. In the wee hours of the next morning, we received an urgent phone call. David's wife, Vi, was in a coma caused by spinal meningitis. We left immediately, seeking God and speaking His Word as we drove straight through to the hospital in Bremerton, Washington. Arthur was given a gown and mask to go to Vi, who was in isolation. When he returned to David and me in the waiting room, I knew God had been present—even before he told us, "The Spirit of God gave clear witness that Vi will be restored to full health."

Arthur headed homeward, not carrying one doubt of God's plan to heal. David took me to babysit the four children, ages 2 to 9, in their trailer located out in the boonies of Kitsap County.

David caught me up with what had occurred Monday, the day before we got the call. "In the early morning, Vi had felt so sick she remained in bed. Because I was in Nevada at the time, Marilyn (9) and Jacki (5) got themselves to school. Carolyn (8), who said she didn't feel well—perhaps uneasy—had stayed home and was caring for Steven, the two-year-old. When Carolyn went to check on her mother, Vi whispered, 'Call Dr. Dean,' then closed her eyes. Carolyn told Mrs. Dean—whose husband had gone to work—'Mom is sick and won't talk to me.'"

My throat constricted as I thought about those little children, their dad away and their mother unresponsive. David continued. "Dr.

Dean rushed away from his clinic to the house, lifted Vi into his car and drove her to the hospital. Then he called me in Las Vegas where I had just registered for a two-week work conference. I caught the first flight home."

All day Wednesday, I followed the protocol David had set up for the children. That evening, he came home with a stirring report. "On my way to the hospital, I stopped to see our pastor, also a strong believer in divine healing, who promised that the evening prayer group would seek God with faith for Vi. Then as I climbed the steps to the hospital, I clearly heard these words: *'I am healing her. You are to tell the attendant in the room, the Lord is healing her.'"*

David took a deep breath, "Those words burned over and over in my mind, and I spoke to no one as I rushed to the Intensive Care Unit. Across the room I saw a middle-aged LPN. God's message burst from my lips. 'The Lord is healing her.' The lady's eyes lit up, and she exclaimed, 'That's absolutely right—that's what the Lord does!' A half hour passed as the two of us shared real incidents of God's supernatural healing. Abruptly, the lady turned her attention to the patient and called out, 'Vi!' My wife's body moved in response—the first conscious act in two and a half days. Then the LPN headed for the door. 'You talk to her,' she said. Within the hour, Vi emerged from total darkness to foggy consciousness, then to the question, 'Where am I?'"

As David finished describing the day's events, I thought about meeting Vi for the first time in May 1960, when our son brought her to our home. He was very low key—as is his nature—so I couldn't ascertain the level of his feelings. However, when he brought her to attend Phil's and Eleanor's high school graduation two weeks later, there was a new gleam in his eyes.

In July—at a family get-together—David had Arthur announce the engagement to Violet Traina. My husband included a detailed dissertation on the benefits of marriage along with a tale of how the couple's courtship jogged into commitment. From what I recall of the story, the two had been part of a running club consisting of the boys in one boarding house and the girls in another. During the course of a few weeks, all the runners dropped out...all except David and Vi. Running slowed to a stroll as the two began to talk and talk and talk—*a well-practiced skill in both of them*! The conversation continued day after day and week after week until our son finally asked Vi about marriage, "But don't answer me now," he blurted before she could respond. "Take the next six weeks of your trip east to think about it and be sure."

She apparently didn't need to think too hard, for three months later, on September 23, David and Vi were married in a sacred ceremony.

Not so sanctified was the mess they came home to from the honeymoon—compliments of David's brothers and those friends from the boarding houses. The co-conspirators not only decorated with the usual toilet paper streamers, they also removed all the labels from the stacked canned goods in the cupboard, smeared peanut butter and Vaseline on surfaces, placed a smoking cigar in the frig, and sprinkled tiny flecks of paper—the minuscule bits from a bank's punching machine—everywhere. For months, the couple would open unlabeled cans and then prepare menus to match whatever they discovered, and for years they would pick snips of paper from pockets and casseroles and books.

I return in thought from the events of the wedding to Vi's remarkable recovery from meningitis. Within one month of her hospitalization, all the David Corey family came to our place. At Arthur's birthday celebration, he asked, "Vi, how are you feeling?"

"I'm feeling so well," she said. "Even gone are the headaches that have plagued me for years. In fact, I am feeling better than I ever have before."

Arthur nearly interrupted her. "Those are the exact words God put on my lips in the ICU: 'Vi, when you come out of this, you will be better than you ever were before.'"

It wasn't until later that Vi realized the words "better than ever before" defined not only the healing from meningitis and headaches, but also from fears that had overwhelmed her since childhood.

God is the Healer. It's true today even as it was when Jesus walked the earth, though so few have faith to see it happen. More on that topic to come in another chapter, but first I want to present a new era of ministry that was beginning in 1971, the same year as the second trip to the Dominican Republic, and Vi's miraculous healing.

PART IV

ROOTS AND BRANCHES
(1971 and beyond)

--SIXTEEN--

With humility comes wisdom

Arthur, by this time, had logged immeasurable miles—thousands by foot and hundreds of thousands by transport. He referred to his ministry as that of a traveling servant or shepherd, and considered his sanctuary to be wherever God landed him—whether in a home, a café, or a roadside repair shop. Perhaps those are the reasons I was incredulous when God wrote a new role for him. He would become the pastor of a local congregation within a brick and wood chapel. As this new calling unfolded before my eyes, I would watch with amazement as Arthur began to accept the differing perspectives and to modify several unbending beliefs. God not only had maturing lessons for me in the senior years but also for my husband.

To place the alterations of Arthur's viewpoint and new role in context, I had to return to the starting point nearly 36 years earlier when Arthur accepted God's commission to feed His sheep. At the time, Art proclaimed he would be accountable to God, and no one but God. If people offered advice, my husband would set that counsel in front of God and seek confirmation of the Spirit. More often, he would seek the direction of God first, and proceed to tell others what God was saying to him. When people expressed convictions that differed from Arthur's, he would quote scripture to defend his position. His perspective may have been biblical, but he didn't grasp how the force of his presentation affronted listeners. In 1947, after one clash in our fellowship, a number of those who were upset left our group. Arthur was dismayed by the fissure between friends, yet the break confirmed to Arthur he was better equipped to minister on the highways and byways than in a traditional format.

Those who left us in 1947 initiated their own study and eventually brought in leaders who helped them establish a church three miles west of us. Over time, Joyce Bible Church became a lighthouse in the community. For us, hurts were healed, friendships rekindled, and new relationships developed.

In the late fifties our children started to attend the youth programs, and Elizabeth became the pianist. By 1971, I was teaching the four and five-year-olds, and Arthur taught a Bible class, led prayer meeting, and preached some Sundays. We hosted receptions or baby showers in our home and summer picnics in our pasture. We seemed to be fitting in moderately well as Arthur steered clear of controversies that could rise from his reactions to the "tenets of ecclesiastical establishment."

That is, until a new pastor at Joyce began to promote membership as a requirement for those who taught. Arthur had always contended there was no theological precedent for joining a church, and I sensed his blood was beginning to boil. *Dear Lord,* I implored, *please don't let my husband upset everyone else by being upset himself.* The Sunday when the message of membership was to be given, we were tied up with so many farm chores we missed the service. I was delighting in the avoidance of an altercation when—to my astonishment—Arthur said, "We will join Joyce Bible Church as members."

I must have looked at him in disbelief, so he explained, "We will be no stumbling block."

It appeared God was teaching Arthur to take his variance of opinion to the Lord and was finding, as Proverbs says WISDOM IN HUMILITY. Once we'd joined, someone suggested Arthur should be Treasurer. Now *that* took some stretch of mind for me to picture my husband—who gives all to the kingdom and who grapples with organizational structure—dealing in nickels and dimes and heating bills. After humorous interaction on the possibility, he declined the position.

Even so, variances of opinion and doctrine were prone to create tensions for Arthur. A merciful God sent Arthur and me out of Joyce Bible to other locations on the Olympic Peninsula. The first new ministry was a group in Sequim named Olympic Gospel Tabernacle. After that, we were invited to Swansonville in Jefferson County, where Arthur initially taught a Bible study and led the singing, while I played the piano. Gradually, he became the primary speaker at Swansonville, and we put down roots.

Tiny, elderly Mrs. Myrtle Swanson was thrilled. She said after years of odds and ends of preachers and no singers, we brought music back to her church—the worship house where she had met

Swansonville Church

and married a young man who'd been attracted to her singing and playing.

Myrtle recounted how her father-in-law had donated the land and materials and had directed the construction in 1904, which I told her was the same year as Arthur's birth. In the style of early century country churches, this one-room temple had a tall bell steeple and a path out back to a one-stall toilet—the latter an eyesore and source of *self's* consternation. Nonetheless, this antiquated chapel was the place of God's appointment.

Organization of the Swansonville group was minimal and sporadic, and the attendance impacted by our nomadic itineration—which included our 1971 trip to the Dominican Republic. Our involvement gradually increased and a few more locals called the Swansonville Church their fellowship, confirming that God had brought us to this community. Thus I was stunned when a letter from one of the regulars was read in our presence on a Sunday morning:

> "As you know, The American Sunday School Union (ASSU) has assisted the leadership of the Swansonville Church and has sent people to fill the pulpit. We have heard from a representative that the ASSU does not approve of Mr. Corey's preaching on the work and the gifts of the Holy Spirit. This representative also said someone from Joyce Church criticized Arthur for being divisive." *(The diary)*

Of course, my defenses boiled up like a steaming geyser. True, Arthur and I—along with relatives and coworkers—had received special expressions of the Spirit, which included tongues or other gifts, but we didn't require others to seek manifestations. Now it looked as if we would soon be dismissed from the place to which God had so recently sent us. My jaw dropped in astonishment when instead of a rebuttal—his erstwhile pattern—Arthur left the matter with the Lord. On Sunday, he read the following statement to the Swansonville congregation:

"We have been told there is disparity with regard to our teaching on the Holy Spirit. Some have said we preach that to have the Holy Spirit one must speak in tongues. This is not our position, nor have we taught that the Holy Spirit always gives gifts according to a pattern or rule. To each of you, I affirm that our ministry here and around the world is only possible because of the anointing and gifting of the Spirit. We, however, do not believe the Spirit is the author of division or dissension in the body of Christ. So it is right for us to resign from ministering in your midst." *(The diary)*

Myrtle Swanson jumped to her feet.

"We have been blessed by the ministry of the Coreys. Much good has been accomplished and I am opposed to Pastor Corey's resignation."

She grabbed a breath and continued, "The American Sunday School group came to our aid when we couldn't find preachers. We are appreciative, but now our circumstances are different."

Mrs. Lund didn't wait for Mrs. Swanson to sit down. "The Coreys have brought the sermon we needed to hear—at least I needed it. I ask that we stand in support."

In the midst of a rousing ovation, she raised her volume. "We can separate from the association if necessary."

Heads bobbed in agreement, but Mrs. Swanson suggested, "We should not be hasty in this matter. Let's tell the representative that we're of the same mind as Mr. Corey."

Yet, the group remained unpredictable and fragmented, and the sporadic offerings scarcely covered our commute of three hours each Lord's Day. When I questioned why we kept on, Arthur said, "God has not sent us away, so we remain."

My spirit was cloudy with discouragement one Sunday when a young lady spoke up: "I have been so alone and depressed. The message Brother Corey brought was just for me."

A sob caught in her throat before she added. "Please pray God will give me peace and joy again."

In hearing her plea, I determined to accept that we were following God's plan and the size and constitution of the group were not His criteria for worthiness.

As time went on, the handful of leaders at Swansonville talked of calling Arthur to be a commissioned pastor. "We'd like you to be ordained," they said. "It will abet our efforts to gain legal recognition by the state and will give you standing with other local clergy."

A man, whose daughter was of marriageable age, suggested, "You would be certified to conduct wedding ceremonies."

Until this era, Arthur had not felt ordination to be expedient and had often argued against its value. To my bewilderment, he approved the proposal, and asked Pastor Bert Linn of Joyce Bible Church to host the service.

The historic weekend started off as a retreat at our place. Friends from Snohomish and other towns came to worship, and some to fast in preparation. Friday evening, March 10, 1972, all gathered at the Joyce Bible Church sanctuary. Rev. Bert Linn led the ordination with participation by the Reverends Oakland Morrison, David Weitzel, William Cross, and Robert Garling. Wilson Myers assisted, and Ruth Myers typed the official documents, which read:

> Being sent out by the Joyce Bible Church, Arthur Wheelock Corey agrees to submit himself to the discipline of the church if, and only when, he may depart from any New Testament doctrine or Truth that may be unscriptural. This will be done only by the governing body of the church. (*The Family Files*)

Ordination Service, 1972

This statement is significant, representing Arthur's new acceptance of accountability with the leadership of the church— Joyce Bible Church!—founded by those who had once left our meeting. This accountability would aid my husband through the ups and downs of ministry from the corners of the Olympic Peninsula at Forks and Clallam Bay across the US, and would empower his shepherding of the Jefferson County flock at Swansonville.

A few more families began to attend our services and brought their children. We conscripted our missionary relatives to speak and our talented children and grandchildren to provide special music. We gave the building a new paint job and enlisted attendees as deacons, naming our group The Christian Congregation. During that season, when travels took us away for extended periods or over weekends, the flock sent us out as missionaries. When we returned their arms were wide and their ears open to hear how God had led.

I was utterly unprepared for the statement Arthur made at the end of communion on Sunday morning, Feb 3, 1980. "The time has come for me to resign."

A gasp swooshed through the room. I was as shocked as the congregation. Yet I'd had similar thoughts. Both of us had been sick; relatives and close friends were in the midst of health and marriage crises; and that morning the commute on icy roads had taken twice the normal time.

"My departure will free you," he continued, "to find a younger man to take over this ministry."

Outcome that day? An outpouring of testimonials and assurances that Arthur's resignation was not accepted. Further consequence was the promise of a salary for us—a monthly paycheck for the first time in 43 years—and of regular donations for two of our missionary families. The following week no spot to park in the lot could be found and the church was bursting. In March 1980, we added an evening service and began searching for a new place. The owners of Forest Hills property, a former stable located across the field from Swansonville church, offered their facility at no charge. It came with carpet, chairs, and two indoor restrooms! Whole families showed up for days of scouring, painting, and decorating. A piano was rented with option to buy. Publicity was in our favor and excitement overflowed to the community. We launched into a new level of ministry…at seventy-five years of age.

--SEVENTEEN--

The Christian Congregation

O ur first service of The Christian Congregation of Port Ludlow was held on Easter, 1980. More than 100 attended, not counting the ladies who were watching babies and toddlers in the old Swansonville Church. Such joy-filled chaos. Many of those who came on Easter returned the following week and the week after. Some were saved and baptized. Others sought forgiveness for having moved away from God.

Mrs. Myrtle Swanson took responsibility to lead music for the children, while I played for the adults and the brand new singing group I named *Joyful Noise Choir.* I also accompanied those who felt *called* to perform special music. Solos brought out the best, but also facilitated the other side of that equation. One Sunday, Mr. Spencer stood to give his testimony which included an impromptu performance. His style was lacking in finesse and his notes missing the pitch. I mentally plugged my ears, thinking, *What a blessing to see how accepting the folks are...after all Mr. Spencer is sincere.* "But," I told Arthur, "when you get to be 92, please refrain from singing solos."

When it became apparent one lady's purpose was to entertain, Arthur asked her to come later for an audition. She left in a huff. Another woman came with her guitar and told Arthur she was ready to present a solo. Arthur said the program was complete but we could schedule her on another occasion. In the meantime, we heard she was involved in witchcraft. "Lord," we prayed, "give discernment to us, your servants."

More folks in attendance translated into more parishioners to check on. We often spent Sunday afternoon calling on new attendees or those who had missed a few weeks. Most lived within a few miles of the church. However, the Whileys, a young hippie-looking couple, lived in a small boat in the harbor. To climb up and down the ladder was disconcerting for this stiff-legged senior citizen! Fortunately, by then my husband had come to corroborate my premise that pants on women were practical, not improper.

Eating and talking and praying with folks—especially when we couldn't take a siesta prior to the evening service—took a toll on our stamina. When there was no better alternative, we dozed in the car or stretched out on the meeting room floor…which suited Arthur fine—he could sleep anywhere. For me, the car was too hot and the floor too hard, but I chose to believe the souls we served were more important than my comfort.

More attendees also meant more people calling by phone. They objected that no one answered to hear their words—a baby born, a concern met, or a request for intercession—so Arthur ordered an answering machine. The recording device accepted every message without a hitch, no matter how many times they dialed us. When we arrived at home from our next five-day jaunt, 14 calls awaited our attention. Off we went again, even before getting a night's sleep. I muted my thought, *Is automatic phone answering really a convenience?*

We added a Monday night youth study and a Wednesday night prayer meeting, and then a Bible Study on Sunday afternoon at Chopsticks, a local restaurant. The owners, Joe and Shirley Tso, wanted us to teach their Korean companions. Christianity for these

Koreans was brand new, so Arthur strained to develop a new vocabulary—one that didn't depend on traditional evangelical jargon.

Arthur was pushing 77 years and commuting five days a week to various communities—some about which I've yet to write. Fatigue was taking a toll on his ministry, and tensions were building. Some congregants wanted more formality, some wanted less. Some disagreed with his positions on healing, while others left without giving reason. I speculated to Arthur, "Might it be you preach too long?"

Arthur asked the congregation if they were in accord with my assessment. "Oh no," Myrtle Swanson said. "Speak as long as you feel led."

The preacher's smirk in my direction told me I'd better keep quiet on the topic. We celebrated Myrtle's 89th birthday. *At that age, I mused, she doesn't have much to enjoy other than the warmth of our group, and—if she falls asleep—the length of the sermon is irrelevant.*

Fewer folks invited us to lunch, so I packed sandwiches just in case. Then we began to have potlucks which Arthur preferred to call Pot Blessings or Fellowship Meals to avoid the word *luck*. He told the congregation, "Nothing happens by luck or chance. God is looking out for us, and the benefits He sends are of His providence."

Not many parishioners stayed in the afternoons, but the food they delivered saved us from Sunday dinner of peanut butter sandwiches.

An ordination and wedding were on the calendar so I took another burden to my husband. "Arthur, the drapes are an abomination. Ugly, unclean, and archaic. We must replace them before these events."

The Christian Congregation of Port Ludlow got an upgrade in time for a 24-hour marathon of ceremonies. First, Arthur led in the ordination of his nephew, Stuart Corey, and one of Stu's associates. We'd barely re-arranged the chairs and it was time to officiate a wedding. In the rush, the pastor-in-charge forgot to get signatures from the four pastors who had earlier assisted at the ordination. So, the next day Arthur drove from Joyce to Forks to Port Ludlow to Bremerton to complete the paperwork, then returned to Port Ludlow in time for the board meeting. The overload for my 78-year-old husband was not good for him, nor for those around him. Arthur lost his cool when one of the more obstreperous board members got off on a tangent. Afterwards, Arthur told me the fellow was "STRAIGHTENED IN HIS OWN BOWELS" which led me to ask, "What in the world does *that* mean?"

I received a lengthy explanation of an obscure biblical text, which I interpreted: Arthur acknowledged his overreaction; the board member accepted the pastor's confession, but took responsibility for his own part; and they are once more in fine favor.

Thus we dealt with our foibles and frailties, leaps forward and steps backward, and inchings ahead again. I wondered, *Can God still use us? Or is the time ripe for us, of our own resolve, to trot out to pasture?*

Arthur proffered to close our chapter at Port Ludlow in July (1982). "We'll trust God to bring a new leader—a younger one," he said.

Some of our best congregants concurred we should retire. Others were not ready to release us, including David Jacobson, who had recently begun attending our church. "Out of the den of drugs, God rescued me," he explained. "When I moved to Washington, I prayed God would take me to one of His teachers. All the way from the biggest congregations in southern California to your little group in Swansonville, God kept His Word!" David drew a breath and continued, "God's teacher for me is Brother Corey. I will take more responsibility to lessen the load on Pastor and help the fellowship move forward."

Mike and Marilyn Hannigan promised to fill more roles, as did Bob Galiottie, who had recently returned to attend services. Yet it seemed God was leading us out. When our day for departure was approaching, we invited the remnant to a picnic by our creek. Fifty came. After the picnic, the board asked us to continue at Port

Ludlow but not work so hard. "You preach the morning message and lead the Bible study. We will furnish leadership for the rest."

Arthur received the clearance from God—we were to remain. Attendance flourished. New believers, longtime believers, rededicated believers, saved-in-the-jail believers. One morning Bob Galiottie asked if there would be an altar call. He explained, "I want to go to the altar to declare I will serve my God in whatever way He chooses."

Arthur stepped down from the pulpit, put his arm around Bob and bowed with him at the altar, followed by a cluster of the congregation who likewise dedicated themselves to serve. Bob Galiottie, a sociable soul, kept his word and brought people from all corners of the community. We held baptisms at the Baptist Church and in Lake Gibbs...baptisms in a spa tub...baptisms in the hot springs...baptisms at the beach. Regardless of the location, we baptized all who gave testimony, Arthur quoting Acts 8:36: HERE IS WATER, WHAT SHALL HINDER US?

Thom Knight, a new arrival during this season, painted a picturesque testimony of what he saw at The Christian Congregation. "Soon after I met the Lord at the age of 53, I was sent to find Arthur Corey's church. The place looked like a redneck hangout with the motley crew that attended: hippies, frumpy old ladies, little kids, and men dressed in their coveralls—some not even clean. Brother Corey could see past the outside stuff to get to the heart of a person."

Thom's impression was valid. Arthur had come a long way in accepting those who weren't clean shaven or dressed in Sunday best. He didn't react to the unkempt hair and beard on a young man named Joe, or the dangling earring on a barefoot drop-by from the boat docks. He simply showed compassion for the hungry who needed God, no matter how they appeared on the outside.

Observers might label our many years at Swansonville and Port Ludlow as topsy-turvy. Several times we anticipated retirement, but were called back. Today, in spite of our humanity, blessings abound and Arthur reiterates, "God has indicated we are to hang in there. We will stay put until God tells us otherwise. We will teach, lead, and counsel as we have for fifty-plus years. We will continue to see God's hand in renewing of hearts, bodies, and minds."

Arthur and Margaret with Myrtle Swanson, 1980

--EIGHTEEN--

Heal the sick

In describing our decades together, so far I've focused on raising and releasing our children, and on Arthur's preaching and teaching and pastoring. I've merely touched on what might be the most impactful outcome of the call to feed God's flock—a spiritual gift of healing.

To delve more deeply into this central part of our calling, I return to the beginning. In the early 30s, after God restored Arthur, his effervescence emboldened others to seek him out. June Marx, whose experience we previously described, was his favorite example of what God could do. In the early 40s, after our arrival in the Joyce community, God healed another barren woman. At the time we met Bill Wetherald Jr and Mabel, they were childless. For nine years they tried to get pregnant. Each time Mabel, a dearest friend of mine, shared with me her burden, I prayed earnestly. Finally I said, "Arthur has a gift I don't have."

At a point of desperation, Mabel pleaded with Arthur to come. He sought God's assurance He had heard the pleas and seen the faith of this couple. In their home, Arthur laid hands on Mabel, lifted his face upward, and spoke to God. Mabel exclaimed, "I felt it! I felt an electrical charge go from the top of my head to the bottom of my feet. I felt it. I know God did it!"

Nine months later, Mabel gave birth to Bill Wetherald III, and—after three more years—to a daughter, Pearl Marie. After Pearl's birth, I had wanted to visit Mabel in the hospital. But my house was full of toddlers and infant Merton, and we had no transportation. So I sent a letter telling her of my happiness that God had fulfilled His promise, not only once, but twice. I signed with these words: AND SHE REMEMBERETH NO MORE THE ANGUISH, FOR JOY THAT A (GIRL) IS BORN INTO THE WORLD.[25]

From the mid-1940s to the 1960s, Arthur's ministry frequently took him away from us. Afterward he would detail the miracles and changed lives, some of which are already documented. During the 1970s, I became a participant as Arthur's reputation as a minister who prayed for people advanced on the Olympic Peninsula. We saw the Holy Spirit touch family members, including our young grandchildren. For example, Janice's child Tony LaRue was just a few days old when tests showed his counts for jaundice were at 16. We were told if they got to 20, he would require a transfusion. Arthur took Tony in his arms and talked to God. At the follow-up test, the number was down to six. Two-year-old Karen Richardson was miserable with the flu when Arthur prayed this sickness would leave. Karen shot her hands into the air. "Hallelujah," she shouted, and jumped down to play.

Mrs. Pratt, a lady from the community, needed God's touch for herself and for her daughter April, whose eyes were so afflicted she couldn't open them. Pastor Linn of Joyce Bible Church and Arthur prayed. Mrs. Pratt was immediately made whole, and April's eyes were cleared. Mrs. Pratt was so convinced of the authority of God that when Arthur was laid up with a serious case of bronchitis—so bad he couldn't preach—she came to pray for him.

Another little April was also healed. Her mother wrote in 1979 on the occasion of our 50th anniversary:

> Our daughter April was close to death from a kidney infection. For ten days, she had been unable to keep food down, and for three days, not even water. She burned with fever and was so dehydrated, her face looked like a skull. I sent for Brother Corey, who brought Pastor Caldwell and Oakie Morrison. As they prayed it seemed as if we were in the Holy Temple and the Lord Jesus was there in all His radiant love. We tiptoed out of the room because we knew we were on holy ground. A few minutes later, April called, 'Mom, I'm hungry.'
>
> She ate four plates of leftover spaghetti and had no difficulty with digestion. In 25 years since that healing, April has never had a kidney problem. Even now I can hear Arthur Corey saying, "Give the glory to the Lord Jesus."
>
> I do, but I'm also very thankful for his servant. *(Mae Erickson)*

Arthur's ministry for healing, along with teaching, extended to other regions. In preparation for each itinerary, whether in eastern Washington, Idaho, Montana, or beyond, God brought to Arthur the names of those he was to contact. Those individuals would arrange for our visit by inviting neighbors and associates into their living rooms, or by scheduling meetings in their own churches.

In Wenatchee we met Jim, an Asian American who was considered legally blind. He felt his way around, wearing thick, heavy glasses. A few days after we had prayed, Jim's wife phoned to say he had passed his driver's exam. Jim introduced us to his associates in the area. One man, Mas Jio, owned an immense farm from which he supplied fresh produce to Safeway and other grocery stores. Mas invited us to his home where we ministered to him and his elderly mother, who said she didn't want to be left out. We also prayed for Tom Sakamoto, who surrendered his life to the Lord. Tom took us to meet his neighbor, Steve Marx, who turned out to be the son of our earliest collaborators Hillary and June Marx. As I noted earlier, June was dying of cancer when Arthur prayed for her. Not only had June been healed of cancer, but also infertility. Steve is one of the children born as a verification of those earliest miracles we experienced. Steve has remained close to us in the years since that *surprise* encounter in Wenatchee.

During this same season, a service was arranged in Anacortes, Washington. A gentleman named Jim brought a lady who'd had a genetic deformity of the spine since birth. Her tail bone protruded, restricting her from normal activity. Tortured beyond endurance, she had become so angry she despised her children. After Arthur taught the Scripture, he and Jim laid hands on the young woman to be touched by the Spirit. The Lord met her in a dramatic deliverance. The spirit of hate left her, and the look on her face as she lifted her arms straight toward the ceiling for the first time in years was a marvel to see. She stretched out flat on the floor—an impossibility for as long as she could remember. Her brother who had the same condition to a lesser degree was similarly healed. These miracles were so unmistakable that a man who had walked away from the Lord returned to faith.

Not all childless families had babies and not all those who asked received physical healing. I often think of our life-long friends Verne and Rene Samuelson. Over the years, God worked in their lives, taking them from skeptical uncertainty to full devotion to the Savior. When Rene became sick, extensive surgery brought no cure, and earnest prayers of faith didn't result in restoration. The day came when Verne said, "If God doesn't choose to heal her completely, we must let her go."

Two days afterwards, I answered the phone. Rene had gone to heaven. When I went to find Arthur, he said, "Yes, exactly at 5:00; I knew God had taken her. Her time had come."

Why does God choose to heal some whose faith is strong, but not all? Why does He heal some with little or no faith? Only He knows.

I will, however, confess to nurturing a negative attitude on one occasion that could have kept others from being healed. We were in the first meeting of an extensive itinerary when I became riled with Arthur's long-windedness. I cluttered several pages of my journal with all the topics and stories he told as he jumped from one to another and went on *Alice-in-Wonderland rabbit trails* with each. I wrote down the time by minutes and half hours which were dragging while I sat and squirmed and sighed and shrugged. I blamed my husband's age and his lack of notes.

God ignored my muttering...thankfully. For I crammed the next section of the journal with His manifestations in that meeting. A pastor was healed of a foot problem that stemmed from a previous injury. A young girl, terrified and shaking, was freed from her fear. A man visiting from a liberal denomination said, "I am a Thomas, a skeptic about this healing business."

The eyes of a mentally disabled child sparkled with new comprehension as her mind was freed. (Subsequently, she was placed in her age group in school and was thriving.) A baby, who had been born *blue* and still struggled at seven weeks, was made strong. A woman whose father had taken her son from her and sent him to an institution was released from the shackles of bitterness. The doubting Thomas, who had watched those have their health restored and minds transformed, blurted: "Now my name is changed again. I do believe."

After Tom's declaration of faith, a man walked forward to the "hot seat"—the chair for prayer. This fellow had been in a serious accident that crushed his voice box. He could only groan and whisper, squeal and squeak. He explained the best he could how as a child, he had felt God calling him to preach but—without a voice—speaking was not even possible. The men anointed him, placed hands on his back and head, and lifted their voices to God. When nothing happened, one of the ministers indicated that the Lord wanted them to move their hands around. The instant a hand touched the man's cheek and another one reached his throat, an utterance of words in an unknown tongue came rolling out of him, followed by full capacity in the English language. (After being healed, this man went on to Bible College. Some years later, John and Virginia McLennan phoned us from Texas. They had met a pastor—unarguably the same man—who exclaimed to our daughter, "Your dad is the one who prayed for the sick and they got well!")

After a high point in the service, we were distracted by an exhibition unlike the *Amens* and *Alleluias* which were expected. One woman was performing a show through raucous raptures and pseudospiritual preening. One of our leaders looked upward and urged, "If this is not from you, Lord, please quiet her."

In a few minutes, she fell asleep.

The following night, a lady about my age spoke. "My life has been governed and bound by the false teaching and evil spirit of Christian Science. I need to be freed by the Spirit of God."

Her face soon glowed from newfound liberation, prompting a well-groomed gentleman to speak up, "I have never been sure of my salvation. I want to know I am saved for eternity."

Once his assurance was secured and his spirit freed of anxiety, he queried, "When do you take the offering?"

Hallelujahs turned to hee-haws, and Arthur said, "We don't take an offering. God supplies our needs through His people who are called to give."

"Well then," said the man, "can I give you something?"

"Try me!" answered Arthur, igniting an outburst of laughter.

We left this location and headed homeward, Arthur asking God to show us someone in the next town who was destitute for a divine touch. At the café, a waitress heard Arthur bless the food. His "Amen" was followed by her "Praise the Lord".

Of course Arthur was geared to converse on spiritual topics. The waitress listened, then asked if we could see her sister who was lame and deformed from rheumatoid arthritis. We knocked on the door of the crippled woman's home, and her teenage daughter opened to us. Arthur expounded the Scripture and ascertained the woman was prepared to trust the Lord. He lifted the crooked legs and waited, first listening quietly for God's direction. When Art felt the muscles soften and her legs relax in his hands, he asked God to touch her joints.

The teenager, mesmerized with joy, watched as her mother's legs evened out. Tears streamed down her face, and she put her hand close to mine on her mother's shoulder. I was overcome with compassion and love for this child who had become her mother's caregiver. I'm sure my tears were as copious as those she shed. We left that family with a benediction and promise of continued intercession.

I'm refreshed and uplifted while reporting incidents of physical and mental healing. However, I feel a disquiet when approaching the subject of the devil and his occupation on earth. Satan wants us full of fear or denial, but God—as I illustrate next—has a different answer.

--NINETEEN--

Deliver us from the evil one

The body, mind, and spirit are inexorably linked—that's Arthur's description. We have seen how healing of the body brings restoration to the mind, or vice versa, and liberation from demonic spirits can transform every part of the person. Yet deliberating on the topic of deliverance is complex. Many in the church today avoid any reference to Satan. Others cede to him excessive power and blame him (or give him credit) for all our failures. Some charismatic circles hold "Meetings for Deliverance" that appear to me as a business or a formula, rather than a gifting of the Spirit.

When Arthur senses demonic influence or possession, he first teaches from God's Word how Jesus dealt with the devil and his legions. He follows with current examples of ways Satan fools both believers and unbelievers through tempting, deceiving, accusing, attacking, or even possessing. "Each time we sin and don't deal with it," Arthur says, "we dig ourselves deeper and deeper into a pit of depravity, hardening ourselves against the Spirit of God. Our sinning yields an inroad for Satan to take advantage and to convince us our sinful behavior is acceptable and normal."

Arthur and his ministry partners—including me—have to be in tune with God, seeking His wisdom and discernment. We pray and, at times, fast until the Spirit clarifies the source of a person's problem. It is God's role to reach into the hearts of the ones who need deliverance and to open their understanding. We are merely servants using the authority given to us by the Holy Spirit. Such was the ministry of deliverance for a young man named Ed about whom Arthur wrote in his notebook:

> I was preaching when Ed blurted out, "Brother Corey, I am being torn to pieces inside while you talk."
>
> I invited Ed to the chair in front, where I and several of the men placed our hands on him. After a moment of quiet, I spoke with anointed authority, "I command every spirit not of the Lord to come out."
>
> A guttural rumble and growling roar spewed from the man's mouth. When the noise was through and the emancipation complete, the man fell over. We prayed he would be filled with the Spirit of God. Ed stood up as a new person. Those present were awed by this loud reminder WE WRESTLE NOT AGAINST FLESH AND BLOOD. The proof was complete when Ed began to share the source of his faith and healing with others. *(Arthur Corey)*

One of our most remarkable encounters with the powers of evil came in the home of a pastor. We knew his wife had been chronically ill and at the edge of eternity when Arthur counseled and prepared to beseech God for her physical healing. While looking to God for wisdom, Art discerned that a spirit was attacking her. "This demonic creature is like an octopus," he said.

"Yes," she confirmed, "that's it!"

Arthur also named the adversary as a leech with suckers seeking to bleed life from its host. So he invoked the name of Jesus to "remove all spirits, parts, and appendages." What a deliverance we witnessed; what a liberation from the tentacles of evil that had kept this woman imprisoned! The source of her disorder had not been physical but spiritual all along. On a subsequent visit, we were elated to see the work had been fully completed, and the woman was free of all oppression. Arthur counseled her to remain on alert. He said, "Satan doesn't easily give up control. You must remember God's Spirit is more powerful than the evil one, and is always available to His children."

In one location Arthur and the local pastor, Rev. Cole, were asked to pray for Tonia, a bedbound preteen girl, who fell into fits of irrational activity. God moved in Tonia's life, taking away all signs of psychotic behavior. After Arthur and I returned home, Rev. Cole phoned, "Thought you'd like to know—an ambulance, two policemen, and a lawyer arrived with orders to take Tonia to the hospital. I told them there was no reason—that she was fine."

Arthur murmured his gratitude to God before Rev. Cole proceeded. "They insisted on following orders but allowed me to accompany her. Tonia was entertained by the fanfare as she walked to the ambulance and then into the facility. I was present during the psychiatrist's examination while he plied her with questions. Within half an hour, the doctor said, 'Tonia, I find no reason to keep you any longer. You are free to go.'"

I want to share one more example. In this case, the release was a process, not an instant miracle. Near Forks, we met Jill and Joel, a couple who'd been delivered of drug addiction, but could barely hold their marriage together. Anger and jealousy would overwhelm at any given moment and one or the other would storm off. We opened our home to the couple and held them close for months. Victory was slow to arrive, but it grew until the day we sent them to Bible school in California. Jill and Joel are a reminder for us TO PRAY WITHOUT CEASING, TO HOLD FAST TO OUR FAITH, and to NEVER GIVE UP NOR GROW WEARY in nurturing God's lambs.

In this warfare with the evil one, we have seen marriages ruined, fathers deserting families, battles waged in the courts, and people imprisoned by addiction or the law. Our role has been to comfort the heartbroken, to succor those who'd been abandoned, and to provide for prisoners of all kinds. As long as the Spirit empowers, Arthur assures me, we will continue to minister to anyone who pursues forgiveness of sin, healing from sickness, or freedom from Satan.

--TWENTY--

Even the wind and rain obey

In the preceding chapters, Arthur and I have portrayed the spiritual and physical outcome of God's call in 1935 to feed His sheep. We were faithful to follow that vision, no matter what ordinary obstacles were allowed to strain and strengthen our endurance—obstacles such as cranky cars, potholed roads, and pinched pocket books. God fulfilled His part of the commission by enacting miracles in lives, endowing us with essentials, and teaching us patience.

With the weather—a less weighty subject—the Master also accomplished His purposes. I wrote in an earlier chapter how, in 1945, Arthur had seen God send clouds and rain to cool him and Hillary Marx. However, the first weather miracle I recorded in my travel diary wasn't until 1972. We'd been with hosts at their dry-as-dust Manitoba farm and had seen their parched fields of grain. In extensive operations like theirs, a severe drought and loss of harvest can leave them buried in debt they have no means to pay. They and their neighbors were on the edge of desperation. We stood in the driveway when Harry said, "Without rain, it will soon be too late for this year's crop."

Arthur lifted his hand, faced the sky, and spoke. In less than half an hour, as we crossed the U.S. border, we were engulfed in a downpour so formidable we had to eat lunch in the car.

In Montana, Bruce Quigley and his wife Joan showed us their drought-damaged fields. Arthur said to God, "You are the master of the winds and the sun and the rain. You have promised to hear when we ask in faith believing. So we are asking you to send rain."

Minutes later we saw clouds forming but moving in the opposite direction. I was reminded of Elijah when he called down rain and saw merely a finger of cloud in the distance. Like Elijah, our eyes were glued to the sky as the clouds turned our way and unleashed their bounty. What a shower of blessing to the Quigleys! The following year, drought returned. On this occasion, God didn't wait for Arthur's prayer to bring rain on the dust bowl. As we drove toward Geraldine, Montana, the showers came with us, proclaiming our arrival. We continued east into North Dakota where we encountered a dust storm unlike any I'd ever seen. Arthur wrote a description in his spiral notebook:

> The high wind and dust churned and rolled toward us, making an eerie commotion. The vast cloud filled the horizon from earth to highest heaven and appeared to destroy whatever was in its path. Daylight turned into blackest midnight. The women in the facility were terrified. "Brother Corey, call on the Lord...Pray!"
>
> But my heart was so full of God's presence, all I could do was praise the Creator and Controller, and declare the psalmist's words: THE STORMY WIND FULFILLING HIS WORD. I didn't under-stand what God was saying, I only knew He didn't give me the direction to pray as the women had asked. *(Arthur Corey)*

I was baffled at Arthur's response to the ladies' plea. He knew God's ability to stop the storm, yet he received no witness—not even a nudge—from the Spirit. The wind moved on, leaving behind dunes of dirt indoors and out, but no major damage. The service continued, after which we helped the women sweep and dust. Was there a lesson in this? Perhaps God had a purpose in allowing the dust to blow. Or, perhaps, He heard the women and moderated the severity of the storm. What I *can* say is that God is in charge and He answers in His way and in His time. This truth is emphasized in the next encounter with untoward weather.

Enroute to Montana in 1985, we discovered the crops were again in peril from widespread drought, and the damage to fields was intensified by an infestation of cutworm. Arthur walked the country road as he conferred with God about the weather and the plague. On the way he met a Hutterite farmer, dressed in his signature black hat and suspender-held trousers. They walked together while the villager opened up with his personal and community issues—which included the damage to crops. My husband was aware that the Hutterites' doctrines focused on following traditions and rules, not on the saving grace of Jesus. So Arthur—after sharing his own journey—urged this unusual acquaintance to take his concerns directly to the Savior. His benediction ended with: "Watch for the rain to arrive shortly. You will know our Lord is in control."

On our next crossing to the east, rain came in torrents while farmers' hay was on the ground. We asked God to stop the deluge and He did. In the direction we were headed a foot of snow had fallen. We rearranged our schedule and headed south. In Texas, we hit cloudbursts stronger than any we'd ever seen in the tropics. The windshield wiper blade on the driver's side flew off and the stick kept on scratching. Large trucks roared past us in the dark. Arthur, unable to see the road, gripped the steering wheel and hunched forward toward the rain-engulfed windshield. Both of us called on the Master of the wind and rain. Instead of closing the skies, He had a different plan. In the dark of night, in the middle of the panhandle of Texas, a service station was open. The manager sent us to a parts store nearby where a replacement was available. We got a wiper, two managers got a witness, and rain went on whacking the windshield. The wind blew us into Colorado where gales had overturned empty cattle trucks, and many vehicles were parked off the road. We made it to a hotel, but went hungry that evening when blustery gusts kept us hunkered down in safety.

The next day we circled back to one of the locations from which we had earlier detoured because of snow. We'd barely shed our jackets when an acquaintance came to see us. Minutes later—in our presence—she received notice her daughter had killed herself. We, who had lost loved ones to suicide, were on hand to minister to this woman and those close to her. God had brought us to them after all the detours and delays of weather at precisely the hour of need.

Some storms hit closer to home, providing other types of opportunities. In 1979, a hurricane-force wind blew through our property, laying down a swath of enormous evergreens and twisting them into oversized piles of pick-up sticks. Throughout the region, winds knocked out power and telephone lines, crumpled roofs, and splintered buildings. This storm also broke apart the Hood Canal floating bridge an hour and a half east of us. For the next several years travel across Hood Canal required a ferry ride, adding both cost and time to any trip east of the Olympic Peninsula. There were long waits and traffic snarls to get to and across either the Port Townsend Ferry or the Lofall Ferry—the latter, merely a small-deck barge.

One afternoon in September 1982, Arthur and I squeaked into the last spot on the Lofall Ferry. As Arthur stepped from the car, a blue-clad official nearby commented. "You were lucky to make this sailing. What a relief it'll be when the Hood Canal Bridge reopens."

I watched the two walk away from the cars, knowing there would be a report of ministry before the end of the half-hour crossing.

I am not equipped to retell what occurred that day, but Arthur remembers as if it happened yesterday:

> When a stranger speaks first, I know God has a message for me to impart. Second Timothy 4:2 says: PREACH THE WORD; BE INSTANT IN SEASON, OUT OF SEASON; REPROVE, REBUKE, EXHORT WITH ALL LONGSUFFERING AND DOCTRINE.
>
> So it was with the man in blue, and I added to his opening words about the bridge reopening. "They expect the Hood Canal Bridge will be completed next month. Took quite a storm to sink the original."
>
> I reflected, "Somehow the wild wind that took out the Hood Canal Bridge three years ago reminds me of the storm in 1940 that caused the Tacoma Narrows Bridge to drop into the Sound."
>
> When the officer raised his eyes in interest, I said, "Because out of that catastrophe in Tacoma I had a most interesting encounter."
>
> "That was a long time ago. What happened?" The official asked.
>
> I reached out my hand to shake his, "I'll tell you what happened, but first let me introduce myself. I'm Arthur Corey and pleased to meet you."
>
> During the handshake, the official told me his name was Frederick, but Fred would do. I repeated Fred's leading question, "So what happened in 1940?"
>
> I took a deep breath. "Well, you see, I am a minister of the Gospel and am often sent by God on errands. In November 1940, the Narrows Bridge collapsed—though I didn't know it immediately. In the night, I received a strange dispatch: *'Catch the Port Ludlow Ferry to Seattle.'*[26] I left before dawn, rode in the bread delivery truck of my friend, and arrived to walk onto the ferry as per the schedule I'd received in the vision. Of course, I was not surprised, for that's always the way circumstances coordinate when God calls and a person obeys."

Looking into Fred's eyes, I gestured with a wide sweep of my hand and paused for effect before adding more details of my earlier encounter. "While scanning the passenger deck of that Port Ludlow ferry 42 years ago, I asked the Lord, *What is the assignment? Who am I to see?* Across the floor, a young man with a military haircut paced back and forth, mumbling, 'There's nothing you can depend on, nothing you can depend on...' Immediately, the voice to my spirit said, *He's your appointment.* I walked up. 'Young fellow,' I said, 'that's a big statement you are making.'"

I waited for a nod from Fred, who by this time was fully attentive. "The young man told me how he, as a new naval officer, had been headed to Sandpoint Base in Seattle by way of the Narrows Bridge on the morning it had collapsed. 'That bridge called Galloping Gertie,' he said, 'lived up to its nickname. A gust of wind and down it went. Can't depend on bridges, can't depend on the government, and don't know what's about to happen anywhere.'"

I looked into Fred's eyes, then said, "The young man's biggest concern, however, was his future. He began to unload his burden that day, as if he'd been dying for someone with whom to speak. He worried about the war going full force in Europe and that officers were being called to their posts. He feared the US would soon be pulled into battle and he couldn't imagine where he'd end up or what he'd be doing."

Fred's eyes widened with comprehension as I moved toward the apex of my story. "The anguish of that naval officer on the ferry from Port Ludlow was my opening to tell him how God had given me peace in place of fear. I'd only begun to give my example to the youth, when he blurted out, 'My grandmother loved the Lord. She prayed for me. And I-I-I should seek to know God.'"

I laughed at the sound of my voice reenacting the outburst of the young officer, and Fred joined in. Then I said, "I agreed with the serviceman that day, 'God sent me to tell you the same thing your grandmother would have said. That you must recognize you're a sinner and on the way to hell unless you turn your life over to Jesus Christ.' The fearful young man nodded in affirmation, and together we spoke of God's plan for salvation and the peace He gives to the person who believes. I continued my mentoring through the first stop of the ferry in Edmonds, and all the way to Ballard."

Fred showed no sign of losing interest, so I continued. "It was time to disembark when the boy inquired, 'Where are you going?' God hadn't given me a destination except that of the ferry, so I hadn't even thought about the other side. But the name of an associate in Seattle popped out of my mouth, 'I'm going to see Axel Fredeen.' When I gave Axel's address, the youthful serviceman exclaimed. 'That's right on my way. I'll drop you off.'"

The Lofall Ferry of 1982 was coming into dock when Fred reached out to shake my hand. "Thank you. Thank you, Mr. Corey, for reminding me to look beyond bothersome delays and accept there could be a purpose I don't know about. I think God brought you today, even as he sent you to that other ferry all those decades ago." *(Arthur Corey)*

So this story within a story was not really about the weather, but rather how God uses adverse circumstances as object lessons. Wherever and whenever, Arthur seeks to be ready in season to open conversations with persons the Holy Spirit has prepared.

Tacoma Narrows Bridge Collapse, 1940 (Public Domain)

--TWENTY-ONE--

Multiple strands strengthen a cord

Readiness in season took on a new sense when Arthur initiated a monumental venture—partnering with other preachers. In the previous forty years, only a handful of associates—like Hillary Marx and Axel Fredeen[27]—seemed to understand his heart's call. But as my husband matured, he sought spiritually gifted team members he believed would fortify the ministry, "Even," he said, "as three strands strengthen a cord."

These partners not only strengthened our branches of outreach, they also gave Arthur…and me…tutorials in teamwork.

In 1970, while we were serving in various capacities at Joyce Bible Church, Bob Garling became Arthur's coworker. Praying for each other and serving people in need, they became knotted as tightly as two ends of a child's shoestring. Was Arthur burdened for one of our youths? Did he seek counsel or fellowship? He'd drop all to call on Bob. Whenever a neighbor sent out an SOS, the two were out their doors in an instant. In fact, if Arthur disappeared without letting me know, I knew what number to dial.

In 1972, Arthur planned a series of meetings in Eastern Washington and Montana, and asked Bob and his wife Pat to join us. The Garlings offered to drive their 1963 Ford Galaxy—an apt idea since we were in an era between functional carriages.

Our friends laid hands on the four of us, and we left chock-full of expectation. The first stop was in Wenatchee where 30 guests, including many Catholics, had assembled in a basement awaiting our arrival. The Holy Spirit reached into our midst, dispelling any divergence of doctrine. We drove on to Ephrata, where two dozen eager listeners scrunched into a trailer. Ross and Wyona Sterling, whom we'd never met before, came to this meeting. A coworker had said to them, "God told me to invite you."

Though tired and hot, the Sterlings arrived, bringing along their son-in-law Don. Afterwards Ross wrote to Arthur describing the encounter that night:

> We had been in a drab denominational church. When you, Brother Corey, spoke the Word, it was like a cold drink in the desert. You asked if there was anyone who would like ministry for bodily healing. When it was Wyona's turn, you asked what was wrong with her. She indicated she had arthritis and one leg was three inches shorter than the other; it had been out of sync since birth.
>
> After praying, you directed Wyona to move her arms, raise them up, and praise God. You picked up her feet and asked our son-in-law to hold a flashlight so all could see what would happen. When the short leg started to come out in length, Don almost dropped the light. That short leg ended up longer than the other one! Everyone was clapping and whooping and praising the Lord. Wyona crossed her legs! That may seem to be a small thing, but for someone who had never done it before, moving her limbs in this manner was as astronomical exhibition. In fact, she spent the rest of the evening crossing and

uncrossing her legs. God did tell the lady to call us for that meeting. Our lives are changed forever. *(Ross Sterling)*

The Sterlings—one example of changed lives—enter later in the account, but for now I return to the partners. We—the Garlings and Coreys—ministered harmoniously in tight quarters, whether trailers or living rooms or basement apartments. Sharing a motel room? Not quite. After the first night together, I noted in my travel journal:

> Too many "personalities" living in close quarters. We should have separate rooms as Pat had said earlier, though Arthur saw no necessity. *(The diary)*

The next night we found a hotel with two rooms remaining. Arthur and I insisted Bob and Pat have the room with a bathroom while we took the $5.00 room with no toilet. Early in the morning, I discovered the community bathroom at the end of the hall was full of patrons. I had to awaken Garlings to use their facilities. To interrupt their sleep for my physical relief measured mortification at 100 percent! After that, we asked God to provide enough offerings for adequate accommodations, and He did.

Arthur and Bob demonstrated complimentary skills in our meetings, but each was a strong, independent character—like Paul and Barnabas in the Bible. In one instance, God took their disparity of style and turned it into a message. We were at a Thanksgiving retreat in Eastern Washington when a man named Jack took exception to point after point of Arthur's teaching. The argument intensified and Arthur couldn't let up. Bob Garling threw up his hands, shook his head, and vacated the room. The slamming of the door smacked an end to the discussion. Then Arthur used Bob's example to explain the passage of scripture: IF THEY DON'T LISTEN TO YOU, LEAVE THAT TOWN AND SHAKE THE DUST OFF YOUR FEET.

Art finished with a warning that God was giving these listeners an opportunity to hear the Gospel and they had better pay attention.

Contentious Jack collapsed to his knees, as did several others in the room.

We'd one day laugh with the Garlings about the Corey penury of room-sharing and the mixed blessing of having rough edges of personality rubbed smooth, all the while rejoicing in lives changed for the kingdom as we co-ministered in the gifts of the Spirit. When Bob and Pat moved away from our community, we missed those collaborators in outreach. They had been faithful to intercede for our children and to pray for me when I was discouraged by the temptations the youth faced, and they had consistently prodded me to keep placing my trust in the Lord.

Cary and Martha Sternback came into our lives in 1972 through Full Gospel Business Men's meetings in Clallam Bay where Arthur had been invited to speak. Rapport was immediate. Not long after, when Arthur stopped at the Sternbacks, Martha said, "I was wondering how to get in touch with you."

"The Lord sent me," Arthur replied. "What's the problem?"

"Can you help a 9-year-old girl in our Sunday school class? She's nearly deaf."

Martha took Arthur to teach the mother and child, and to pray. Seeing no immediate results, he urged the girl and her parents to believe for a miracle. A few days later in a different town, this girl was in attendance. While ministering to the needy, Arthur suffered a deafness he'd never felt before, as did the other guest speaker. Art wondered, *Is the deaf spirit that's afflicting the girl wielding Satan's influence over others in the room?* Assured of God's direction, Arthur opened to the Gospel accounts of Jesus and the deaf spirit. While he read the Word, the ears of all three were cleared.

On Arthur's follow-up with the little girl in Clallam Bay, Martha's face lit up to see him. I have to add my own comment: I'm not surprised God's love shines through Art to those who could do with an uplifted spirit. When the person is an attractive young woman, I can tease him, "No matter how old you get, you still look good to me too."

Martha's husband, Cary, also became a coworker. He had accepted the Lord in a church in Clallam Bay, though he said, "I never heard the gospel preached there. God had to reach me on His own."

As Cary grew in the Lord, Arthur suggested that he become a minister. "I can't," Cary said. "I have a terrible temper and foul mouth over which I have no control. It's been a problem all my years as a logger."

Art said, "I know all about temper. Mine has caused offense on many occasions. Even today, people may preface their comments with, 'Now don't get mad, Arthur.'"

Cary initially struggled in his walk with the Lord, but he counts Arthur as the one who made him aware of the requisite to know the Word of God and to live accordingly. This friend has a sense of humor that has made their visits a pleasure for us. For example, they would sometimes pass our road on the way to Port Angeles for groceries, and Cary would ask Martha, "Shall we stop in?"

If she didn't want to, he would joke, "Do you have sin in your life so you don't want to see Brother Corey?"

Also stopping by for mutual ministry and companionship during this era, was a young couple, Louie and Gayle Lee. They and their colleagues, the Bakers, were from the Forks area, about 30 miles from Clallam Bay and about 60 miles from us. Louie—once a timber-cutting, tough-talking logger—had met the Lord, quit drinking and smoking, and brought twenty others to Christ. At Louie's invitation, Forks was added to our regular itineration list which—by this time—included Swansonville, Clallam Bay, Full Gospel Men's Fellowship, home meetings in Joyce and Port Angeles, as well as groups in Eastern Washington and beyond. We were ministering five nights in a row, traveling the state, and calling on folks during the intervals. Age and aches were catching up with me and my spirit drooped. Though my emotions weren't in agreement, God gave me the strength to discipline my mind through repetition of the verse: *MY STRENGTH IS MADE PERFECT IN (YOUR) WEAKNESS.* When I kept my eyes on Jesus and off the pressures of activity, God helped me tag along with Arthur and his young logger collaborators.

Arthur values Louie's contribution as a spiritual partner and gifted servant of the Lord. We appreciate his talent to communicate the gospel of God's love, and have been blessed to have him and his group join us for ministry in many places: the gatherings in our home, The Christian Congregation at Port Ludlow, the home group of Clallam Bay, or even across the ferry to Whidbey Island.

Whidbey Island is home to another couple who have partnered with us—Stuart and Laraine Corey. Arthur's nephew Stuart (Stu), son of Harold and Vera, was transferred from California to become Lieutenant Commander at the Whidbey Naval Base. On a lagoon, near the facility, Stu and Laraine purchased and remodeled a home. In the 1970s, Stu and Laraine inaugurated a Tuesday night study attended by neighbors, acquaintances, and guests from wherever. All welcomed Arthur's messages, embracing him as Uncle Art and me as Aunt Margaret.

Like the folks at Swansonville, Forks, and Clallam Bay, the Whidbey gathering blessed us before our trips, and upon our return reveled in the results. Excitement would build long into the night as Arthur never wearied of repeating stories. I admit I often propped open my eyes, fixed a smile, and hoped my head wouldn't land on my collar bone.

Laraine, Stu's wife, was active in Women's Aglow—the women's full-gospel association. She started a family camp program and hosted regular retreats for which she asked Arthur to speak. These assemblies included hours of singing and preaching and interceding. I twitched with discomfort during demonstrations that knocked people to the floor, and my Victorian sensibilities prickled with all the hugging that went on. But I recall the restoration of one couple whose marriage had been splintered. These two anchored their arms around each other as Arthur baptized them at the Whidbey pool.

Stuart retired from the Navy in 1978 after a full career. On Whidbey, he set up the Corey Oil Company, which has opened many additional avenues for influence, and he continues to be a congenial, strong, and personable witness. Stuart, our giant-in-spirit nephew has motivated many to a closer walk with Jesus, including Arthur and me.[28]

The preaching partners previously introduced tended to subscribe to Arthur's exacting evangelical position that we are saved by grace but must live as Christians by fundamental biblical principles. This viewpoint had earlier steered Art to be strict with our children, at times censorious of me, and ever resolute in the requirements he took upon himself. But God was teaching Arthur (and me) that even as He has saved us by grace he continues to engulf us with love and acceptance no matter what mistakes we make.

The next partners of which I write are examples of such grace. They have befriended us in spite of our peculiar ways. And they have helped us see beyond religious creeds that once would have clattered our *conservative* convictions to hearts that Jesus loves.

--TWENTY-TWO--

Be all things to all people

As I looked back through my years of record keeping, a neighbor's name kept popping out—Rose Tieche. She has known us as well as anyone might...and loved us anyway! She has forgotten our failures and our propensity to create tension among the saints. Rose was present in the '40s when the fellowship broke away from our place, but never held it against us. She and her mother were available in the '50s when Marian showed up at their door—running away from home—and they kept our 10-year-old safe until she was over her gloom. In the '60s and '70s, Rose helped me prepare for wedding showers or special birthdays I hosted. "I'll make cakes," she'd say, and proceed to bake, not any saggy flat cakes, like the kind I made, but masterpieces of art and culinary indulgence.

Rose has given me rides when I asked for them. She has hosted Bible studies, served as treasurer at Joyce Bible Church, drawn up our insurance plans, and helped us manage finances for our ministries. Always level headed, capable, and compassionate, Rose continues to bless us.

My next example took us in another direction toward grace. Gladys, a dear friend and widow of many years wrote to us that she planned to marry Don. We knew Don's wife had divorced him, and were surprised that she would even consider marriage. *Was she making a decision contrary to God's will?* People around us quoted the scriptures which, of course, we knew by heart. But Arthur didn't answer the counselors. Instead he went to his corner for God's direction. He wrote to Gladys, "You must find the assurance for yourselves. I cannot tell you."

When Gladys wrote of their wedding, questions circled in our heads, but we asked the Lord to bless their union. I wondered later, did Gladys and Don prepare us for the breakdown of two of our own children's marriages? How earnestly we had yearned for our daughters' reconciliation with estranged spouses and prayed for those men who had rejected Him. Yet *grace* would not allow us to ask our loved ones to reenter relationships with the wayward ones who had abused the marriages through infidelity or desertion. When potential second marriages came into discussion, Arthur could answer his daughters, even as he had responded to Gladys, "We can't tell you what God desires of you. We will pray, but you must know His mind for yourself."

Back to our friends, Gladys and Don. God blessed them, and blessed us through them. No matter if they had organized a meeting—which they usually had—or if they were out in their work, we could walk in their door, find food in the fridge, and a bed made up. Come morning, Gladys would give us haircuts and pack us a lunch for the road. They were colleagues and servants of kindred spirit.

Besides those of our own Christian creed, like Gladys and Rose, others have come into our lives from entirely diverse backgrounds. We partnered in Spokane with a Catholic clergyman whom Arthur depicted as a "called one whose heart is honest and committed to the Lord."

Arthur held the funeral for a Jehovah Witness man who had years earlier requested him to speak at his graveside. God knows if he was ready to meet the Lord, but we know his burial allowed for a gospel sermon to all who were present.

A Mormon, whose son's marriage was breaking up, came to Arthur for guidance. This opened another doorway to witness that Jesus, who is Savior and not merely a holy man, could bring relief and renewal.

Among those who have blessed us, Verne Samuelson, a partner from as far back as the late 30s tops the list. For decades, Verne had been the respected owner of the Samuelson Ford Motor company in Port Angeles. He had been a community frontrunner who was active in Moral Rearmament, a philosophical movement that contends the world would be at peace if leaders would live moral lives. After years of Arthur's teaching him that *all* have sinned and must seek the Savior, Verne comprehended the truth. He then opened his living room for Arthur to lead weekly meetings attended by individuals of many denominations and doctrines, as well as those with no beliefs at all. Verne became part of the Full Gospel Business Men's movement and took Arthur to their events. As a result, FGBM organizers often invited Arthur to preach and to minister to those who asked. At one of these meetings, Arthur sat in front of his full plate of food, not touching a bite, neither before nor after he spoke. "Aren't you hungry?" His neighbor asked.

Arthur responded, "When I entered the room this morning, the Spirit spoke these words to my spirit: *'There is an adulterer in this room.'* Immediately came the verse: I AM WRITING TO YOU THAT YOU MUST NOT ASSOCIATE WITH ANYONE WHO CLAIMS TO BE A BROTHER OR SISTER BUT IS SEXUALLY IMMORAL OR GREEDY, AN IDOLATER OR SLANDERER, A DRUNKARD OR SWINDLER. DO NOT EVEN EAT WITH SUCH PEOPLE."

Arthur continued, "As that mandate rang in my ears, you can be sure I lost all hunger for food...even this gourmet dinner and dessert."

God didn't reveal to Arthur who was guilty. Instead, God spoke to the man, a highly regarded Christian leader. The following day this executive disclosed the truth to another who'd heard Arthur's message, "I'm the one of whom Arthur Corey spoke. I have been cheating on my wife and engaging in an affair."

Verne's high level connections and Arthur's attention to the voice of God resulted in this man's repentance.

Verne didn't introduce us solely to the high and haughty. In 1973, he took us to meet the Whileys in Port Gamble near the Swansonville church. This unconventional couple I mentioned earlier was living on a boat in the harbor, and cooking with another couple under a campground roof on shore. Duane Whiley had studied for the Catholic priesthood but became disillusioned with what he considered tradition without significance. He had delved into various cults and eastern religions, eventually showing up at the Port Gamble Episcopal church. Through our encounters with Duane, he and his wife gave their lives to the Lord. The former doubter and cynic became so excited in his newly-found faith and enlightenment, he brought his priest Father Carney to Arthur. This Episcopalian minister asked Arthur to teach him how to use spiritual gifts in care of his flock. Such a unique background, but what an open mind!

Duane Whiley also queried what God had to say about raising funds to cover the Episcopal Church debt. Arthur recounted his calling and the verse he lived by: SEEK YE FIRST THE KINGDOM OF GOD AND HIS RIGHTEOUSNESS, AND ALL THESE THINGS WILL BE ADDED. Whiley explained the verse to Father Carney, and the priest wrote a homily for his congregation. He concluded his message with a statement that raised my eyebrows, "Pastor Arthur Corey is a saintly man and I have learned much from him."

Father Carney's flock responded to the request and the obligation was covered.

Saintly Arthur Corey?!

Yes, I agreed, *saintly* in honoring the Lord, *saintly* in living by faith, and *saintly* in learning to accept those whose interpretation of God's Word doesn't quite line up with his own.

But, oh my, not so saintly when fretting over the IRS.

Arthur Corey at Joyce Bible Church, 1964

--TWENTY-THREE--

Faith and the IRS

Every year! The tension builds, the frustration grows, and the sleepless nights increase. Arthur wrestles with his numbers—the donations, the expenses, the deductions—and his perception that the government is determined to outwit him.

Arthur has always been meticulous in his data keeping. He has documented every mile driven in ministry, every gallon of gas used, every cent of expense on the road. Yet the IRS never seems satisfied without a question…or an audit.

One year, at the audit, the agent looked at our papers and questioned, "This lengthy excursion to California brought in only $20 of income, but you deducted hundreds of dollars in the travel expenses? Your deduction is entirely out of line with your stated income."

Arthur explained our commitment—that we went without expectation of funding. The agent shook his head. I, however, was armed with the specific journal and showed my record of the places we'd stopped. Arthur said, "We went for the purpose of counseling a couple whose marriage was falling apart. Don't you think it worthwhile to go all the way to California to save a marriage?"

The agent must have accepted the validity of this explanation for his attitude reversed and he became our advocate.

Another year we returned from travels to discover a bold alert on the blackboard, IRS WILL CALL TOMORROW. When the call came—after a twisted-pillow night—we learned the error on our part was simply a missing number.

On the other hand, in 1978, the IRS sent word we were being audited for our filing of three years earlier. For two hours we pleaded our cause, our accounting, and our income. The agent's big deal this time—at the end of it all—was to tell us we could only include meal deductions if gone more than one day. We celebrated the end of the interview by eating a *nondeductible* meal at Haguewoods, after which Arthur added columns to the book for meals we could *not* claim.

The dread loomed sooty-black on each spring horizon, long into the 80s. Arthur read the Bible, offspring quoted verses, and Bob Richardson teased him. When my husband faced the IRS, no brotherly advice brought him serenity. Arthur fumed and fretted and fussed, "The government is a giant of a brother. They're going to deride me and intimidate me. They'll say, 'Nobody gives away that much!'"

Indeed, I thought, *we give away the resources in our hand or in our account. Our children are in missions, our loved ones lack necessities, and those we've discipled are in Bible school.* "But," I said, "it doesn't help to worry."

Phil's wife, Darlene, followed up with, "It's okay, Dad; we'll visit you in jail."

Her bit of humor brought a temporary release of the tension...until we got word we still owed $300.00. In his message on Sunday, Art said, "My relationship with the IRS has resurrected again. It is alive, but definitely not well."

Later in the service—as a call to the unsaved—Arthur asked that we sing the first two verses of *My Faith Looks up to Thee,*[29]

I requested, "May we also sing verse three: *When life's dark maze I tread and griefs around me spread*...because..." I paused, "Pastor Corey treads such a dark maze of the IRS."

The day after, Arthur collected his records and left them with Don Bell, a CPA, who turned over the last of the documents to the IRS...after telling us we owed a coffer more. *God bless the Men's Breakfast Group.* They gave Arthur a check that more than covered the amount. My comment to Arthur, "I'm remembering the ever-present co-op bill when we were gravel-pit poor. The hassle of the IRS seems less worrisome to me than the lean years."

Wouldn't you know, the small salary fostered a cargo ship weight of anxiety when the IRS confronted Arthur for receiving regular income and not paying Social Security obligations! The fine was $400.00. Arthur explained to the agent that he had opted out in 1937 when the Social Security decree became law. "I was not on salary and was permitted to sign away both obligations and rights."

"I find no record," the representative said, "that you opted out then. Furthermore, opt out wouldn't count anyway, now that you are on salary."

We paid the fine. The next year, Social Security surfaced with a dictum we owed $1335.27 plus interest, calculated back to 1980 when salary had begun. That night, I awakened to hear Arthur making a racket in the living room. I called out, "A.W.!" (I only used my husband's initials when I was not amused.) "What in the world are you doing?"

A.W. showed me a sign he had posted. THIS IS NOW MY STUDY. I was sure an office in the living room would do nothing to alleviate IRS and Social Security angst—not even provide an additional deduction—but the dither-laden activity gave him a project to accomplish while his insides were in turmoil.

The Social Security issue couldn't be avoided any longer. We were instructed to see Mr. Tuck at his office in October. Arthur kept track on the calendar and at 8:00 AM on the first of October we were ready, a full hour ahead of office opening. Our son-in-law, Dennis Alwine, went along to defend and bolster. He did much more. When

Arthur wanted to explain the opt-out clause he'd signed 47 years earlier, Dennis shushed him, "Please go with the flow, Dad."

My husband was silent as Dennis questioned the agent, "If Arthur is supposed to pay into Social Security for the three years he's been on salary, shouldn't he be receiving monthly payments starting the year he became eligible?"

Our son-in-law paused for effect. "In my calculations that should be more than ten years."

The official stroked his chin. "You may have a point there, but let me check."

He left the room to discuss the matter with his supervisor, and returned to declare, "You are right. The Coreys will pay the portion required and fines for the last three years. They will receive a check for the total of back payments from the date they became eligible. When the paperwork is complete, Social Security will begin sending a monthly disbursement in the mail."

We would celebrate a solution we'd not seen coming, and an answer to the prayers of a man whose faith was stretched beyond its sanctified limit at tax season. But first, I looked at Dennis and turned to Arthur, "Wow, now we can support three or four more missionaries!"

--TWENTY-FOUR--

Let Arthur be Arthur

For the man of faith, dealings with the IRS were a test. Another test would come with illnesses that didn't flee when prayer was lifted...particularly when the one afflicted was Arthur. My husband had seen God heal multitudes and had experienced miracles in his own body. Thus he expected God would always honor his unwavering faith and guide him by divine voice or specific verses as he awaited healing.

One example came from his 60th year, after he had injured his shoulder. For weeks he kept his arm secured in a sling. He regularly conversed with the Lord and had his associates surround him for prayer. Each time he tried to use the arm as an act of faith—or resistance—the ache and the sling returned. One morning his attention was alerted to Psalm 74:11: WHY WITHDRAWEST THOU THY HAND, EVEN THY RIGHT HAND? PLUCK IT OUT OF THY BOSOM. The context didn't match his convictions, nor was it about healing, yet he took the order as God's command to him. He pulled his arm from the sling, threw it straight up in the air, and shouted, "Praise the Lord."

Arthur put his arm back to work, as if it had never been lame. God had not delivered the answer at the first request, nor at the second, nor at the third, but rather in His sovereign schedule.

On another occasion, Arthur awakened with a headache and fever—not unlike a bug that had gone through the community. When I asked if he had the flu, he countered, "I'm not sick!" Then added, "I just had a rhema."

"What, for evermore, is a rhema? You appear quite ill to me."

"A rhema is a word or utterance from scripture. And the rhema I received—and am uttering—is found in Isaiah 33:24: THE IN-HABITANT SHALL NOT SAY, I AM SICK."

I didn't bother to ask about the biblical context before he explained his position. "Therefore I shall not say, 'I am sick.' Instead I shall choose to reject whatever is trying to undo me."

Arthur had a drawn out, restless recovery from that *not-sickness*. Bob Richardson and Louie Lee came to pray for the strengthening of his muscles and the uplifting of his soul, and that he would soon be recovered from *that* which had lowered him to his bed. Sagaciously, they avoided the word *sick*. And Arthur eventually recovered from the virus.

As a band of twelve—plus extras—living in cramped quarters, we had faced many afflictions. Seven-year itch, ring worm, mumps, measles, chicken pox, Asian flu. After the children traveled to other locations, they returned bearing mononucleosis, hepatitis, malaria, parasites, food poisoning, or…you name it. God has brought healing through many forms: His divine power, the wisdom and medications of His servants, or just time and rest.

An ailment that has beset me my adult life is a gimpy knee. I injured the joint while hiking on Mt. Rainier in the 1920s. Since that fall, my clumsiness in slipping, twisting, or tripping has resulted in recurrences of stiffness and swelling. My leg has remained crooked in spite of prayers, and I've walked for most of my life with a glitch and a limp. But, *thank you Jesus*! I've not needed a wheelchair.

On the other hand I took note of the twinges in Arthur's back, his shoulder, or his arm that were caused by excessive hours repairing equipment, hauling hay, or chopping wood. I surmised these aches were not a *sickness*, but an inability to use ordinary sense in his senior years. One recent New Year's Day, Art, after hobbling for weeks due to various stitches and spasms from overwork, said, "I hope you don't think me delirious, but will you go on a jaunt with me?"

My initial reaction was, "Are you certain you have the witness of the Spirit? I'd like to verify you're not suffering cabin fever caused by your besetting tendency to do too-much-of-too-much."

I reminded Arthur of his heart attack years earlier after which he'd had been stuck in bed for weeks. Healing had been a process, a discipline, a choice, not an instant divine act. I assured him, "You don't want to repeat that process…nor do I."

I've wondered, *Might the man of faith be subjected to physical misery as evidence that God has his methods and timeline? Should Arthur be more empathetic when the faithful don't see immediate restoration to full health? Choose not to link their illness to sin, to lack of faith, or to oppression of the evil one?* These are questions not fully answered for me.

While the anecdote of my husband and his rhema might amuse us—the significant truth is that he believes God's Word. The Master Healer has honored Arthur's prayer of faith by healing young, old, and middle aged; by raising up the terminally ill; by giving babies to barren women; and by enabling normal capacity in the minds of mentally disadvantaged children.

Meanwhile God has continued to instruct Art, even while on his bed of infirmity, that He—God—is sovereign and chooses to act according to His design. Arthur needs to let God be God. And I? Instead of nurturing a critical attitude need to let Arthur be Arthur!

PART V

HOME TO ROOST—NOT QUITE
(The 1980s)

--TWENTY-FIVE--

Welcome the multitudes

Through all our years of travel and ministry, home is where we have found our respite…at least until crowds arrived! Our ten children, their spouses, and offspring—the latter of which I have nearly lost count—all gravitated to the place of their roots. They brought their friends, those friends brought *their* friends, and we put out the welcome rug for all. We found space to bunk the visitors—regardless of their numbers—in the barn, on the floor, in tents. We fed the multitudes. Our children got married and returned with their own kids in tow, so we ran a daycare center for the young ones so older ones could go fishing, hiking, camping, hunting, whatever. A note from 1963 represents dozens of similar entries:

> What a morning…steady downpour. All Virginia's kids, my younger ones, and Micki and Dennis (Richardson) are housebound. The noise is a dull roar when it is not a complete roar. *(The diary)*

Family Gathering, ca.1963
Back: Arthur, Margaret, Jeanette, John, Bill Richardson (R), Dave with Carolyn, John McLennan (Mac)
Middle: Stacey Raub, Edward Raub, Ricky Halpin, David Mac, Dawn Mac, Micki R, Janice, Elizabeth, Vi, Virginia, Star Mac
Front: Marilyn (Dave Corey), Dennis R, Dina Mac, Daniel Mac, mid-1960s

To accomplish pending jobs, a contingency of laborers showed up. They butchered animals and packed meat for the freezers. They laid a new roof, built a deck, installed insulation, constructed a drain system, or repaired all of the above. Parties supplemented the work. Scrabble games and jigsaw puzzles were added to shelling peas, canning fish, shucking corn, ending beans, freezing berries, making jam, mending clothes, cutting hair, giving perms, and eating popcorn. Afterwards we went out to dine using coupons Janice collected. Or we gathered in the back dining room of the Chuckwagon near the organ and piano, where we could sing and share without distraction. Most often we pooled our food resources and feasted at home.

When our international children and grandchildren returned, celebrations were planned or they spontaneously erupted. We met at SeaTac airport or reunited at a sibling's home. We accompanied the missionaries as they spoke in various meeting places. I, for one, didn't want to miss the hymn sings, jamborees, or reunions that could include multiple families for several days...or weeks. If Arthur received a travel directive when the cadre of kin was assembling, he'd sometimes give me a special dispensation. "I can go without you. Enjoy your tribe and *all* the chaos they bring."

Arthur's birthday also became a basis for festivities. At first this party was an extension of Christmas, in deference to his contention we were to celebrate God, not man. However, by the time Arthur reached the big 7-0 on December 27, 1974, he had outgrown that concern. He couldn't argue against Elizabeth's lemon merengue pie, and even now declares he is happy to be honored all year long with such a pastry, whether made by Liz, or Debbie, or Marian, or whomever.

Around 1983, as Arthur grew in his appreciation of get-togethers and could see the amount of labor involved, he suggested an upgrade in the kitchen to facilitate feeding the armies. I said, "We do just fine."

As he extolled the virtues of a microwave, I argued, "It's an unnecessary expense."

My resistance hit corked ears, and Arthur recruited a crew to corroborate his cause. "Okay, I fired back, "I get to donate equal amount to sponsor an orphan."

I found use for the microwave—to warm up half-cups of coffee I found in the bathroom, the bedroom, the laundry room, or the basement. I really had to keep track of those cups as they were a sign to my husband I'd become dependent on the caffeine, and he ought to preach me a sermon on addiction. Hurrah for the micro-wave...and fewer sermons!

When the microwave died in the middle of Thanksgiving, the season of hunting and butchering and house repairing, I had to eat my earlier complaints. *How in the world would I feed the armies without that fast cooking apparatus?*

An *attitude* also beset me when—during another hectic spell—a dishwasher was discussed. "With all the hands in this household, why for heaven's sake do we need a dishwasher?" I grumbled. "But go ahead, just go ahead and buy the machine. Our missionaries can use that much of a boost in their finances."

Soon I questioned how I'd ever managed so many years without a dishwasher.

Arthur didn't dispute my compensatory donations. When he purchased a tape player for the car, the Sudan Interior Mission received from me a matching gift. When he purchased cassettes for *his* player, I felt compelled to send a donation for Famine Relief. When Arthur ordered a rug to go with new linoleum Merton had installed in the kitchen, I sent another contribution. Arthur appreciated the benefits of possessions, and his wants helped feed the destitute.

My children told me I should learn how to accept a gift. After their admonishment, Arthur bought me an automatic coffee maker on my birthday, and I chose to be such a meek recipient that no one got an extra donation. Seemed a shame! Next I was *courteously* thankful when Merton bought and installed an instant hot water tap at the sink. I was *honestly* thankful when I discovered I could have an instant cup of coffee, and Arthur couldn't keep track. Now, instead of thinking about money and expenditures, I choose to think how blessed I am to be part of this selfless bunch.

Our basement has become a storing place for all sorts of stuff—not our possessions, but furniture and appliances and clothing and memorabilia of family members in transition. We can see missionary kids' keepsakes along with their parents' appurtenances that didn't find another parking lot before flights took off for Timbuktu. "Thanks," they say, "for storing this stuff someone might want...*someday*."

Arthur rejects excess encumbrances. He has been known to trash historic artifacts, such as his dad's antique clock that David subsequently salvaged and promised to fix. Or, he has ignited a bonfire with the full intention of burning articles no longer in use, such as my mother's 1800's treadle sewing machine that Darlene rescued. When she questioned Arthur's intent to clear out the storehouse, he shrugged, "Nobody will want this junk."

Worried about the household items and toys about to disappear in the flames, Darlene called Marian, "Come to the rescue. Dad's on the warpath against the clutter."

When I heard about the incident, I said to my offspring and their progeny, "Go right ahead and fill the basement with trappings, because it means you'll be back, and the sooner the better!"

Arthur had to agree, "If it *really* means you'll return sooner and stay longer, then leave it all here."

However—just in case the need for order got the best of him—he posted a disclaimer he had lettered in bold, permanent red ink:

NOT RESPONSIBLE FOR GOODS LEFT OVER 30 DAYS. (OR ANY LESSER TIME FOR THAT MATTER!) HAVE A GOOD DAY! WE LOVE YOU.

Then he gathered his tackle and cap, hooked up the boat and trailer, and went fishing.

Arthur Goes Fishing, ca.1960

--TWENTY-SIX--

He goes fishing

Fishing had started back in the 40s when Arthur fashioned gear from a stick and a string and a bent pin. The boys added a squirmy worm and skipped to the creek for trout. In the 50s, when Bill Richardson married our daughter Elizabeth, he and his dad Bob delivered to us a wooden boat with outboard motor and tackle, and became fishing mates and mentors to our teenagers. At the slightest suggestion, our gang would head for the Straits of Juan de Fuca, and—during seasons of plenty—everyone who held a pole in the boat caught seafood which we ate, canned, froze, smoked, and shared.

For summers in high school and college, our youth were employed by the owners of Crescent and Agate Beach to assist the patrons of the fishing resort. One of the guests, owner of a well-equipped fishing vessel, sometimes waited for Mert to get off night duty at 5:00 AM so they could fish together. From one such trip we have picture proof of their proficiency—several immense halibut weighing in at a total of 600 pounds. By the time our boys went away, Arthur found himself hooked on the sport.

In 1961, Bob Richardson and his wife Ruth moved as missionaries to Alaska. With his buddy Bob away, Arthur began to build his own fleet. His first boat and trailer were a gift from our neighbor, Mrs. Tieche—who was always thinking of ways to encourage him—and his first motor came from Tony Sunseri of Snohomish. Arthur no longer had to wait for an invitation to get out on the water.

A season or two later, after a series of repairs to boat and motor, Art envisioned a new boat and trailer and motor and tackle. Some friends sent a monetary gift following the sale of their property, and he assured me, "This is perfect timing."

I said, "Go for it."

What was I thinking? Or was I *not* thinking. With his new gear, Arthur took to the water with gusto. Those who went along could expect to remain in the boat from daybreak to sunset even when nothing was biting. Our grandson Dennis was about 12 years old when Arthur invited him and gave this caveat: "Now you are not to complain that you're bored. Do you understand?"

Dennis muttered to himself, *Grampa will see how tough I am. I'll not cave in first.*

The fishing had been unproductive and the hours long and dull for Dennis, when the skipper finally said, "I think we have stayed long enough. Let's go in."

I stewed when Arthur wore his dress pants and returned smelling like a fish monger from the wharf. I envisioned the worst when he went out alone and wasn't back by dark. "If you are so concerned," he said, "you can go with me."

"Right," I replied. "I could never land the salmon if we snagged one. I definitely don't want to be as bushed as you are at the end of the day."

His fishing was a cross to bear, and I growled about it. Finally, since I couldn't change or manage him, I joined him—partly because I wanted him off the water at a reasonable hour, and partly because he wanted me along. I was rewarded. On my first outing to Freshwater Bay I netted five of Arthur's catches and, on the second day, I caught two fish of my own.

For those fishing excursions, we drove about three miles to Freshwater Bay at the best tide. Art would situate me in the boat, release it from the trailer into the water so I could secure it next to the dock. Arthur parked the trailer, climbed into the boat, and we trolled out to sea. On a profitable trip, we caught a salmon or two and a few bottom fish before we followed the reverse order on our return. This protocol functioned until I reneged. The weather was frigid. I couldn't sit that long in one position. There was not even an outhouse on the ocean. Etcetera!

With his *conscience* no longer facing him in the boat, Arthur would again linger from early 'til late—until his back ached so much he couldn't stand straight. He'd limp up the steps and put off cleaning the catch. Of course, whenever another potential shipmate showed up, he'd straighten his spine and head out.

On the other hand, when Arthur's buddies came over and verbosity defied my endurance, I'd push them out the door. "Here's a snack," I'd say. "You can stay out in the boat as long as you like. But a platter of salmon would be nice for supper."

With one of these accomplices in the boat, Arthur caught his trophy fish! That Sunday at church my husband, Brother Corey, put on a cabaret-worthy show. As he portrayed the event, the excitement in his voice gave way to motions of his limbs. He jumped from behind the pulpit and extended his arms. The buttons on his suit coat strained against the button holes, his white shirt showed at the waist, and his tie bunched up. "I'd never felt anything like it," he said. "Even wondered for a moment if I'd snagged a whale."

Arthur's left hand squeezed an imaginary pole that flailed every which way, while his right hand circled as if winding a reel. He added, "I could see the gleam of reflection as the fish swished next to the boat and charged out to sea."

The preacher, hanging onto the invisible tackle and nearly collapsing on the floor, inhaled. "But I persisted, didn't let go. Eventually the 30-pound salmon quit the fight, and I could—with the help of friend and net—drag him into the boat."

By the time the act was over, the congregation was in hysterics. They'd never seen their staid and serious pastor put on such a spectacle. Well, I hadn't either and thought perhaps he'd stepped beyond the boundaries of propriety.

Arthur returned to the pulpit and waited for the uproar to subside before turning the tale into an admonition. "It's God's way with us. We may be loaded down by the weight of sin; we may have rejected God all our lives; and we may expend our last smidgen of strength to get away from His boat. But He loves us enough to hold on until we get the point."

Pastor paused before continuing. "Of course, God never forces His will on us, like I did to that fish. He wants us to know that our sin is not too heavy for Him to forgive, nor our rejection too strong for His grace."

Arthur grew tired of skippering a boat—too strenuous for his aging body. Friends offered to buy the entire ensemble. *Thank you, Lord!* My husband did, however, keep a canoe near the pond in our yard. He had stocked the water with trout and had been feeding them for years. One day he snagged a blubbery trout he couldn't land. Not anticipating potential consequences, he stood up to improve his pull. He improved his pull alright—right over the side and into the water with hook, line, and fish! When he came up from the bottom, the catch was attached to his line and a lily pad crowned his bare head. Once again, he put on a dramatic re-creation in church to a howling audience and a hide-her-face wife.

Arthur never lost the love of fishing and even yet is quick to accept an invitation from Bob Richardson who, after 10 years in Alaska, moved next door to Bill and Elizabeth.

I interrupt myself to offer an accolade to Bob Richardson. Bob has been an ally like none other and to my knowledge Arthur and he never argue. When my husband is edgy, Bob can disarm him with a quip. They spend hours scrutinizing scriptures, feeding each other's faith, and reaching out to neighbors. And, of course, reminiscing about the fish they caught…or the *big* one that got away!

God has used friends like Bob to stir us toward deeper consecration. I thank the Father also for the multitudes not named who have served us in their dwellings, at their churches, along the byways and waterways…or, at our place on the farm—this spot on Highway 112 called home.

--TWENTY-SEVEN--

A place called home

In 1937, we set up housekeeping in a weather-wearied grange hall on one quarter acre. In 1946, we dismantled that building and repurposed the scraps into our farmhouse on a 21-acre piece. Finally, in 1958, we moved into our real home—the Big House. Now, nearly twenty years later, this place is a refuge for Arthur and me... between the floods of folks who come. But the farm on which our home stands didn't start out simply or quietly.

We grew a garden with patchy success. We planted a chef's stew of carrots and potatoes; managed a marketplace supply of poultry and eggs; cultivated barn-stuffing acres of hay; and canned a castle larder's stock of berries, apples, and plums. We raised animals worthy of Old MacDonald's farm: chickens, ducks, geese, pigs, goats, cats—though not all at the same time. We bred cows that gave milk, but got milk fever. The cows gave us calves that kicked up their heels and broke through the fences to devour the gardens we'd sweated buckets over. Our youth battled caterpillars and daisies and thistles and dandelions. I get weary merely thinking back over those decades that could fill an almanac of guesswork farming.

The last of our family moved on and we moved out in ministry. The land was left with weeds in place of garden rows, fences with no cows to control, a barn stashed with stuff instead of hay, and a larder loaded with fruit canned a decade earlier. The final animal to leave us was Duke, our pet dog. Duke, dear Duke—an oversized black lab who acted like our children—loyal and independent. When Arthur and I were traveling, we'd leave him at Elizabeth's. Inevitably, within a few hours he would trot the three miles home and be waiting for us. On one weeklong trip we got as far as Port Ludlow—more than an hour away—when we discovered Duke in the trunk. We left him with Nick, one of our parishioners, but when we returned, Duke had disappeared. We drove homeward sensing the loss—almost as if another of our children had left for a foreign land. Duke showed up the next day at Nick's and we were reunited. I surprised myself by crying with joy. But Duke was sluggish, half blind, and beyond dog years. One day a neighbor delivered his body from the highway to our porch. It fell to Arthur to bury him. For months I glanced out the kitchen window or watched from our car, expecting to be greeted with his wag.

Duke was gone, the land had no farmhands, and our outbuildings were deteriorating as steadily as their owners. *What,* we pondered, *would become of the property when we could no longer manage the simplest of maintenance? Or when God would call us to heaven?*

Our children had similar concerns and told us so. Some suggested a retreat center or a Bible Institute, while others said the property should be an inheritance for all of our children. "Think of the ones in ministry," they explained. "Those kids have exchanged earthly earnings for eternal riches."

In 1979, on the occasion of our first family reunion,[30] we established a trust. The property was divided into legal sections to be purchased by those who wanted a chunk of the homeland. They would pay into an account for our retirement years, and we would remain as long as we wanted, or for the rest of our lives. We would retain a base for our missionaries—even overlapping two or three families if their furloughs coincided—or provide a short-term shelter for the locals.

As soon as the legal papers were signed by the land recipients, they got busy. John planted trees on his acreage. Marilyn and Allen designed a remodel of the abandoned farmhouse—until practicality won out over sentimentality. They sold their portion to Virginia and John McLennan.[31]

Phil and Darlene took ownership of Grandma Phenicie's house which was known as the "Little House." When they arrived for furlough from the Dominican Republic, they had a home. When they were gone, we rented or loaned to pastors, visitors, and down-and-outers. We were responsible for maintenance—repairs, septic issues, invasion of ants. I was always relieved when my children and their families moved in and were stewards of the bungalow's well-being. First came Janice and her son Tony, then Merton and Debbie. When the Alwines brought their three *cherubs* (plus one part-time) to live, I doubted they would fit. Dennis said, "If you, Marian's mother, could live where you did with your tribe plus extras, we can make do in Grandma Phenicie's house."

David and Vi invested in the family home and surrounding land. How convenient for us to have a landlord. We could take the maintenance issues to him—the leaky roof, the faulty basement bathroom, the broken steps, and the termites! He'd say, "Fine, take care of it," and Arthur would hint that he, David, owned the place. Thus the landlord arranged for us to take the cost of materials from the rather small rent we paid, after which he or Mert would bring a crew.

Payments began arriving from the plot owners and piling up in the account, which—added to the pastoral salary—was building a nest egg like none we'd ever had. True, if we didn't need it, the money would be inheritance. "But," Arthur rationalized, "the Lord might return any day, so we and our posterities will have no need for a store house of mammon."

On that basis, Arthur withdrew money to purchase an electric typewriter. I was not in accord with the cost, but he would not be dissuaded. Once I got used to the feel of the keys, my record keeping improved. The machine was a lemon and before the year was up, we returned it twice for repairs. The third time the company furnished a new one which lasted long enough for me to figure out where the keys were. "No more complaining though," I told myself, "simply be grateful."

As our account grew, Arthur wrote checks for each of our children. We were reprimanded for cleaning out our retirement, but I thought, *$600 to each of our ten will cover gifts for birthdays and graduations I missed because I had nothing to give.*

The account also allowed us to put down payment on a vehicle for Dennis and Marian to replace the Jeep that was dangerous, wide open to the weather, and clumsy for tucking their babies into car seats. Arthur bought a lawn tractor which he drove off the bank, almost into the creek. When I asked if he had prayed regarding this purchase and this job, he said he always prayed; then he acknowledged, "Well, maybe not about this *one* project."

Arthur hired our grandkids for odd jobs, and even paid the going wage…whether or not the thistles got eradicated. I was glad he could sponsor them in ways we could never assist their parents when they were young.

God has endowed us with all these things—a place to call home and ample income to supply our daily bread, plus extra. It took eons in earthly years, but He promised and He fulfilled.

In defense of earthly years, by this time my husband and I had assembled quite a few. I would remind him I am the "old gray mare who ain't what she used to be." Arthur, however, acted as if he were still a kid in rubber boots. He'd quit counting candles.

--TWENTY-EIGHT--

Is 80 the new 40?

"And guess what?"

That's what my Alwine grandkids say to grab my attention. Do they ever love to tell me what "guess what" means! I used the same expression when I wrote a letter to my sister Eleanor on the occasion of Arthur's 80th birthday:

> And guess what! Now that Arthur turned 80, he has gone out to sled down the hill with Marian and her youngsters. They wanted me to go, but *self* feels no obligation to act 40 when my knees don't carry my weight and I'd need an excavator to extricate those knees from the deep snow at the bottom....Love, Your Sis

Arthur's party was a monumental affair with family uniting and well-wishers stopping by. The Christian Congregation hosted an event and gave Arthur a gift certificate for $80.

Celebrating Arthur and Margaret

At 80, Arthur grew a beard the ladies said made him look young and distinguished. I said he acted slightly vain about the new image he presented, and suggested the extra hair required more mirror-facing than 60 years of shaving. For *my* new look, Marian gave me a permanent. I checked the mirror to discover the curls didn't thicken the wispy hair—a genetic gift from my mother. The facial creams I got from Elizabeth didn't smooth out my sagging skin, and the new clothes Janice bought me didn't begin to camouflage my shape.

Neither of us looked any better after a makeover than before. This hopeless concern over appearance propelled me back to a decision I've regretted ever since the day we were married—I'd permitted no photographers at my wedding. What a pity not to have saved a 1929 likeness of the newlyweds to pass on to posterity. I didn't like my looks then, but I wasn't contemplating the image I'd present 55 years later.

Arthur also attempted jobs meant for younger guys. I heard a racket in the living room and discovered he was trying to install a ceiling fan by himself. "It will be easy," he said.

"Not at fourscore years," I said.

Art ignored my opposition. A hefty plywood fell on his head and he moaned, "A bolt of current just struck behind my eyes."

My independent husband sat down and waited for a son to come by and finish the job. He also postponed washing windows and cleaning the chimney until a young man named Mark Thomas arrived.

Soon after that, Arthur had his first-in-60-years physical and his head was fine—only a bruised knot remained. His ear test showed he had hearing loss, which I already knew since he missed much of what I said to him. His blood pressure measured normal. *How can that be,* I marveled, *given he preached twice on Sunday; conducted a board meeting and two Bible studies at Port Ludlow and one on Whidbey Island; participated with Full Gospel Business Men; mentored leaders of Women's Aglow; and went to see folks in Forks and Clallam Bay? All in one week!*

When I went for a checkup, my hearing also measured low, but my blood pressure measured high! I asked for more rest on Sunday and— *Thank you Jesus!*—the afternoon Bible Study at the Chopstick restaurant was disbanded.

As Art passed his 81st birthday in December 1985, he felt a burden for his remaining siblings who had not assured him they were ready for heaven. We went to Fox Island to see Jim Corey, who was virtually deaf. Jim assured us he was prepared to meet the Lord and was looking forward to seeing his parents on the other side. Jim's funeral was held on July 12, 1986, ten days after my 81st birthday. At the memorial, we were thrilled to find a younger generation eager for Arthur's witness. Only Arthur's brother Albert seemed reticent to discuss eternity. As had been his response for years, Al thanked Arthur for his prayers. We are confident that those petitions will be answered in God's way and in His time.[32]

The summer of 1986 was exceptionally loaded. John and Jeanette and their five girls came to stay while they prepared for their daughter Melodie's wedding in Seattle and for their own return to Liberia. Ron and Eleanor brought their kids from the mission house of Emmanuel Bible Church where they were based during furlough.

At our place, grandkids and belongings overstuffed every nook and niche. But I didn't hear grumbles of boredom. The youngsters had learned long before that "I'm bored," was an invitation for me to give them a broom, a mop, or—if the timing was right—a bucket to pick berries.

In the midst of the pandemonium of a dozen teenagers or more, invitations for Arthur and me continued to arrive. No way could he turn down an official invitation from Mr. Oas, the SeaTac airport chaplain, to attend a banquet for those interested in the airport chaplaincy. The initial connection with John Oas had occurred six years earlier when we had gone to pick up Rose and Mrs. Tieche. Their flight was delayed and we met the chaplain. "Rather by accident," I recalled to Arthur.

"No," he said. "By divine appointment."

"Okay, you finish the story," I said, and he did:

> When we met him, John Oas was in need of inspiration. Inspiration is my specialty, so I gave him my best. On a second occasion at SeaTac, while waiting for my grandson to arrive from Alaska, I felt an urgency to look up Mr. Oas again. He was thrilled to see us, saying, "I have wanted to talk with you."
>
> "Well, here we are," I said.
>
> After that, the all-expense-paid invitation to the upcoming banquet arrived in the mail. My wife complained she had nothing to wear, but we went anyway.
>
> John Oas stood and asked me to join him on the platform. Both of us told of the earlier encounters, and John added, "I wouldn't be in the chaplaincy today if Mr. Corey had not given me the guidance of God, to 'keep on keeping on.' Whenever it seemed I was making no difference in my ministry, that reminder would come and I could keep going."
>
> *(Arthur Corey)*

Mr. Oas reserved us a plush suite where we discovered we were too wound up from camaraderie and coffee to sleep.

I'd not even recuperated from the banquet and subsequent insomnia when Arthur was ready to go again. He told the church elders we needed a sabbatical, and one chuckled, "Fine, it will give us a little relief."

So in September 1986, John and Jeanette left for another term in Liberia, and we took their daughter Reenie to school in California. We continued our itinerary, missing one preplanned meeting when Arthur couldn't find his glasses. Providential in my thinking, for this would have been a Bible Study prone to foster confrontation. By the time the class ended, Arthur found the glasses in the car where they had been all along. "Not a sign of age," he said.

I agreed, "This was God keeping the peace."

The waylaid glasses led to a discussion of all the locations we'd had to backtrack to collect our Bibles, our coats, his razor, his briefcase, or my purse. Forgotten items, however, were a minor theme I found in the epic records we have gathered. No, the overriding thesis would read like this: *Arthur was anointed for this service. God blessed many, and it was so right.*

We'd barely unpacked our travel bags when Arthur said, "The Lord has revealed we must go to eastern Washington."

Upon our arrival in Ephrata, our hosts showed us an article in the paper about the murder of Marcia, a young woman we had known. We went right away to the grief-stricken Sterlings who'd fostered Marcia for several years. She had left their home, quit school, and married a guy she had known four days. When she received an inheritance soon after, the husband squandered it all. (He later pleaded guilty to the murder.)

God had told Arthur to go *now*. The timing of our arrival allowed us to minister to these friends precisely at the time of their need—an attestation to the accuracy of God's clock.

The trip to see the Sterlings was our last tour prior to my illness. This means I have stitched my crazy-quilt collection of memories from the 1920s to November 1986, when the empty space recorded my six-week sojourn of silence.

This also indicates I will soon close my journals and set aside the letters—those testaments to God's supremacy in our lives. God was clear in issuing the call to Arthur and persistent in teaching me to trust. To Arthur, He gave guidance, and to me, stamina. He prompted my husband to moderate his temper and tongue, and helped me replace fear with faith. The Father honored both of us by bringing to Himself the loved ones who initially rejected our message, and by allowing us to see the fruit of witness wherever He sent us. But God's favor of priceless value is the treasure of our ten children serving Him and loving each other.

To all of them, and to those who'll come after I'm gone, I dedicate these shards of reminiscence. May you be encouraged to walk faithfully with God, listen to His Spirit, and trust Him for the ones you love.

When the angels call me—won't be long now—I'll be ready. They'll not carry me to a grange-hall shanty, a stick-and-stone shack, nor a kitchen full of pots and pans! Instead, they'll lift me to a song-filled mansion and into the presence of Jesus. *Oh, that will be Glory for me.*[33]

--TWENTY-NINE--

Postscript

But not yet! I was ready, but—as of March 1987—there's been no call. You should see the twinkle in Arthur's eyes and the spring in his shoes now that I have stamina to accompany him on a victory-over-death tour. He has the brand new Crown Victoria parked out front, but the engine is not running. God has not told him "*Now,*" so he is quite amenable to my request for leeway.

"Please," I ask, "before we leave, may I tuck into this collection of memories a few of our old letters? Don't you think our descendants will appreciate the symbols of our love for each other these sixty years?"

My beloved picks up a letter, dated 1968, and across his face spreads the grin of a newly-married young man.

--THIRTY--

Love Letters

From Arthur:

Husbands, love your <u>wives</u>...Please dear, don't misinterpret the plural word for wife. Because you know you're the only one. And besides that, this is the easiest commandment I ever received from the Lord, and I'd sure like to be able to give expression to the feelings I have for you right now.

Well, enough of this sort of thing, how can the Lord be able to use me if I go around lovesick, and my desired one is better than a thousand miles away. So I'll steel myself, or rather, BRING EVERY THOUGHT AND PURPOSE INTO CAPTIVITY TO CHRIST.

A week later he wrote:

> Surely don't dare to dwell too long on thinking about you or I might under such weakness consult the map on the quickest route home. Well, I deliberately wrench my mind from such thoughts. Except to warn you I have put on five or ten pounds the way I've had been fed. Now do not misunderstand me. Fact of the matter is, I'll be glad for the most meager of fare and have my dear one by my side. (There I go again—help us!). Tell Mert hello and I'm not so sure I want him reading my "love" letters. He could get some dangerous ideas, and he's pretty young yet...

My response:

> Dear Husband of Mine,
> This is a Red-letter Day: I got a letter from my boyfriend. And I was so pleased to get it. Seems like a LONG TIME you've been gone.
> No, I'm not really living it up. Just out with the Hawkinsons once to Denny's for pie and coffee...and you know how they keep filling the cups, without keeping track. There is a Penney's store in walking distance from the kids' place in Ballard. Once I went in alone and came home with a new two-piece dress. Boy – I hope you like it???!!! Cost $7.88 (marked down from $10). I'm thinking of going back and getting me a nightgown. Should I get a sexy one?
> Love from your favorite wife...M

Arthur followed with a special envelope, poem, and insert:

> "What can I get my love to show
> How she affects my heart?
> A broom, a mop, a pan, Oh No!
> This would abase the part.
> Ah ha—a light doth now appear,
> (I've struggled long and hard).
> Dear One, please use, without reserve
> This Penney's credit card."

I answered with:

> I just had an offer to go to the grocery store. Of course I would like to, but I only have $1.29 cash and $4 in the bank account. Guess that won't allow for much shopping, that is OK anyway. We are still eating. (Penney's card not accepted at the grocers). Yesterday, I got $10 for teaching piano lessons. Need to pay the phone bill, but also want to put $1 in the missionary offering for the Pennoyers. So then the phone bill will have to wait.
>
> Sunday, I sat in on adult class you usually teach. Guess what! I like you better.

Finally, for our anniversary that year I sent him a store-bought card engraved with this verse:

> People seem to think our honeymoon is over...well...
> They've never been married to you.

EPILOGUE
by
Eleanor Corey Guderian
Stanwood, Washington
2020

Margaret's life was far from over in March 1987, when she settled into the Crown Victoria next to Arthur. They traveled extensively during the following two-plus years. The miles piled on and the years took their toll, but Arthur kept moving. Margaret noted in a travel log: *Arthur says this may be the last time here.* A few months later, on a return to the same location, she wrote down his comment: *I thought we were done here.* In a third entry noting a similar stretch of territory, Margaret wrote: *Arthur remarked for the third time in the middle of North Dakota he's not going to instigate these safaris anymore.*

In between trips, Margaret and Arthur continued to host home guests and pastor The Christian Congregation of Port Ludlow. They kept close tabs on their posterity, and welcomed Raman to Bill and Elizabeth Richardsons' family, Jonathan to Dennis and Marian Alwines' family, and Alana Joy to Merton and Debra Corey. The Alwine family later grew to include Megan, Joshua, Sarah, Matthew, and Dennis's older daughter Annie. Mert and Debra also became the parents of Lydia Grace.

In 1989, Margaret sensed her body was failing. In July, though suffering, she attended her 60th wedding anniversary celebration and the family reunion. Soon after, she had surgery for removal of a large tumor in her abdomen. Margaret, my mother, never fully recovered. During the following months cancer spread.

I traveled from Ecuador to be part of the 24-hour care we shared among family and close friends. On June 25, 1990, I was singing the words of Psalm 23: "YEAH THOUGH I WALK THROUGH THE VALLEY OF THE SHADOW OF DEATH, I WILL FEAR NO EVIL, FOR THOU ART WITH ME"…when she lifted her hand to welcome the angels who'd come for her.

221

Arthur, my father, soon appeared as desolate as the Mojave Desert—except for the oasis of God's presence and the occasional visits or plates of food from the locals. Gone was the whirlwind and hullabaloo of clan coming to care for his wife. A photo taken of Dad shows drooping shoulders and weary eyes. Months after Mother died, I caught a flight from Ecuador to spend a few days at the home place.

Our second morning together, Dad danced to the kitchen table. His eyes glowed like luminescence in the ocean as he told me of a vision he had seen. "I looked up from my bed, and there was Margaret standing at the foot. I had to blink a few times to ascertain I wasn't also in heaven."

A smile crinkled his cheeks, "There she was, dressed in a shimmery green dress, the young, beautiful woman with whom I'd fallen in love. It was as if she wanted to assure me she was young and healthy again, and we'd be together forever."[34]

Margaret and Arthur, ca.1975

AUTHOR AFTERWORD

Readers of my first book often asked, "When will you tell the rest of the story?"

I had published *Sticks, Stones & Songs—The Corey Story*, to recapture for posterity the adventures of ten hardscrabble siblings and our parents in rural Washington from the 1930s to the 1950s. During the research process, I amassed cases of notes from multiple sources and voices—volumes more than three chronicles could hold. So I chopped and cropped and condensed, noting the *rest* would have to be told at a later date. That later date arrived when I caught the vision to unify the historical account of Arthur and Margaret Corey—focusing on the years before and after the decades charted in *Sticks, Stones & Songs*—to provide a record for their successors, now numbering more than 200.

As an author-in-progress the second time, I transcribed additional decades-old cassette recordings and interviews. I googled names of my parents' associates and friends, and found most listed in obituary columns. To my delight, however, a handful of oldies could still talk of their remembrances. I have taken editorial liberty with their stories as well as letters sent to Margaret and Arthur in honor of their 50th and 60th anniversaries and have included some in the text or in the End Notes.

Here I pause to acknowledge the assistance of David Jacobsen, content editor and mentor to this novice. He understood the significance of documenting the history of Arthur and Margaret Corey. His honesty helped me determine what was relevant and his perspective clarified for me what readers would experience.

I gratefully recognize Shelby Zacharias for her proofreading attention to details of grammar. I take full responsibility for any errors I added after she completed her review. I give thanks to Elizabeth Dolhanyk for her skill with graphic design of the cover and her patience while I made up my mind; to Darlene Corey for fine-tooth combing the manuscript more often than should be asked of relatives; and to my husband Ron for taking several turns with the editing pencil, and for allowing me the freedom to dedicate the past three years to this endeavor. Appreciation goes to many others, including Mary Kimble and Icle Crow, who encouraged me with affirmations and valuable suggestions.

In this parenthesis, I also salute the people who gave my first book, *Sticks, Stones & Songs,* a voice in their communities: folks from the Historical Societies of Port Angeles, Forks, Tacoma, and Marysville, Washington; libraries in Clallam, Jefferson, and Snohomish Counties; bookstores, churches, and senior communities; as well, as my second cousin Diana Krieg Goodman, who continues to give and sell and promote on our behalf.

As the first draft of Margaret's story came together in 2017, I asked my siblings to review the content. *Did the voice sound like that of Margaret? Was the portrayal of Arthur and his ministry accurate? Was I free to include the tales of her children as told by Margaret?*

The last question was vital, particularly for my brother Merton. He honored me with permission to include our mother's perspective of his pilgrimage as a testament to the faithfulness of God. On October 25, 2017, Jesus took Merton to Glory. My brother's sudden departure left family and community in shock. Yet we are comforted to know his voice is providing clarion tenor tones in God's Praise-the-Lamb Choir, alongside his brother-in-law, John McLennan, his brother, John Corey, and the family's faithful patriarchs, Margaret and Arthur Corey.

END NOTES

[1] Margaret's illness was caused by a systemic staph infection that initially appeared as inflammation in her wrists and ankles. The lesions on her lungs, which were not biopsied at the time, disappeared. In her diary, she never named the infection. Margaret's concern about a possible stroke was written to her sister in a letter.

[2] Frank died of "quick consumption" (perhaps tuberculosis); Cal of tetanus; Frank of diphtheria; Emma of a sudden unknown illness.

[3] Charles Kent Phenicie, Family History, compiled in 1995. Current maps show Edith Creek and Myrtle Falls. Another Edith, Edith Corbett, also had a role in the history of Mt Rainier. She was the second woman to reach the summit. For this writing, no official record of the naming of Edith Creek was located.

[4] Arthur's mother, Anna Corey, wrote in January 1928, that her husband, Merton, accompanied Arthur to Fox Island for his second radio marketing trip.

[5] George Bennard, *Jesus is Dearer than All*. Words and music ©1914.

[6] Information on Dr. Roy T Brumbaugh confirmed in writings of David T Myers, Aug 20, 2012 and Aug 20, 2015, and reposted in Aug 22, 2017, for the online archives of *This Day in Presbyterian History*. Brumbaugh's group that met in the Scottish Rite Cathedral was initially known as The Independent Bible Church. Later the name was changed to Bible Presbyterian. An internet search revealed that this congregation moved to a new location in 2017 prior to the demolition of the Scottish Rite Cathedral.

[7] Eleanor Corey (Guderian) inked those scrolls into her first book, *Sticks, Stones & Songs—The Corey Story*, an account of the ten Corey children, their parents, and a scruffy community during the 1930s to 1950s. Laura Frantz, best-selling and Christy award-winning author, wrote the following: *Sticks, Stones & Songs* offers a rare glimpse of a bygone era and the people who made the woods of the wild Pacific Northwest their home.

[8] John's and Jeanette's story has been taken from the book, *Any Ol' Bush Will Do: The Life Story of John Corey* as told to Jim Morud. Permission granted by John's wife, Jeanette, and their daughters for the author to include this story. Some words and phrases are provided verbatim, others edited for space. *Any Ol' Bush Will Do* is available through Amazon and other outlets.

[9] In a short window of time, Allen Thompson retrained the faculty to teach academic courses he had adapted from his learning at Columbia. Allen also focused on helping students develop their own cultural-appropriate leadership and governance.

[10] Allen Thompson wrote a follow-up report on Cuba at the request of the author:

> *As soon as Castro declared himself a Marxist, Cuban pastors were sent to reprogramming sites similar to concentration camps where they endured hard labor for several years. Upon release they returned to their churches, reopened the Los Pinos Nuevos (LPN) seminary which had been closed for five years and continued ministry under harsh circumstances.*
>
> *In 1978, I was given permission by the Cuban government to revisit the Island to celebrate the 50th anniversary of the founding of the LPN seminary and denomination. I found a struggling church weakened by relentless restrictions and Christians suffering under constant cultural opposition. A 'suffering church' continued until the fall of the Soviet Union in 1989. In 1990, under economic pressure due to the loss of Russian subsidies, the Castro regime began to court the evangelical protestant and Roman Catholic churches. Many restrictions were lifted, the disgrace of being a 'religioso' faded, and public religious discourse commenced. From that date to the present, Cuba has experienced a religious awakening with one million (10% of the population) now claiming to be evangelical Christians.*
>
> *In 2008, I was asked by the leaders of the LPN denomination to assist them in a process of spiritual revitalization and church expansion. As a result we have helped the believers begin a program of non-formal lay training focusing on understanding and applying the gospel. Training centers have been opened across the Island and over 5,000 house churches started by participants of this training. Life-on-life gospel coaching introduced in dozens of churches has brought new depth to the Christian experience. A modern printing press has been imported from the Dominican Republic and the printing of Bibles and religious literature not available before is now in continued circulation. Music and art fills the churches with praise to our God. This is God's doing.*

[11] David Livingstone was a famous pioneer medical missionary in Africa in the 1800s. The quote is by Stanley, a reporter.

[12] In May 2018, the book *"The History of Onchocerciasis—River Blindness in Ecuador: From Discovery to Elimination"* was published in Spanish at the Central University in Quito, Ecuador. This scientific publication documents the research that Ron Guderian began in 1976, as well as the methods of intervention and treatment that he and his team conducted during more than 20 years.

In 2014, the World Health Organization certified the elimination of Onchocerciasis in Ecuador, and since then, in other countries that used the same protocol. More information on Guderian's work and publications is available on the internet or from the family.

[13] Phillip gave this report:

> In the dark, Darlene and I with our Mark, Melanie and 3-month-old tiny baby Tim were traveling from Florida to Washington when the engine of the loaned Chevy station wagon blew. A long wait beside the road ended when a camper stopped. The couple helped us get Darlene, the children and a box of frozen meat onto a bus.

> The next day, I located a phone—no cell phones then—to call the owner of the car who would wire the money to pay for a junk yard engine we had located. Next, we went in search for a mechanic, all of whom were hanging out incognito at the rodeo. Meanwhile, the money was sent to a bank at the wrong town. At 11:00 PM Saturday I left to travel 400 miles across the prairies with no sleep and no radio, but with a seal that leaked a quart of oil every 100 miles, and no stations open when the needle of the gas gauge sat on empty for eons. I, half-mast, arrived at the church where Darlene was preparing to simultaneously talk, show mission slides, and hang onto three traumatized kids.

> Darlene told me their bus had arrived in Sheridan where she was to buy tickets for Great Falls. She was short of cash and, as the baby screamed, the bus driver handed the agent $20, the amount lacking for their ticket. At the next transfer stop she crossed the street to Denny's restaurant, poured water from the hot carafe to mix with formula for Tim's bottle, and a stranger handed Darlene money for their breakfast.

[14] A few notables: Merton grew in church leadership responsibility after returning from mission assignments, serving as deacon and elder. In 1995, Mert and his wife Debra helped her sister Neva launch the AWANA program at Joyce Bible Church. To date, 24 years later, the program continues, and local children are learning scripture and coming to understand God's plan for their lives. Mert has led numerous work teams comprised of relatives and members of Joyce Bible Church to Chile where they worked with his brother-in-law Terry Thompson, and to the Dominican Republic. He also took teams in 1994 and 1995 to Ecuador where Ron Guderian served as a full-time missionary until 1998. More than 20 years after Mert completed the team projects in Ecuador, the results still speak out:

Phillip: *I recently accompanied Ron Guderian to Ecuador. Biggest thing in my mind was to see the hospital Mert had brought teams to build. We traveled all day by canoe up the big river. The hospital, about 100 feet by 40 feet, stood on posts 7 feet above the ground, and at least 18 feet up the bank from the river. When Ron and I arrived, the people were delighted to see their Doctor Ron. They also remembered my brother Mert—"as a strong, inventive, and courageous man", who had come to help them build a hospital to serve their people, both Chachi Indians and Afro-Ecuadorians. As I toured the place, one local guy unlocked the pharmacy to show me the shelves and a small stock of medicine. In another room the hospital administrator—who is also a dentist— stopped working on a young person's teeth to welcome me.*

Ron: *Years before the work parties began, the locals and I planned the construction, cleared land, and calculated the amount of lumber needed. Using five chainsaws, which supporters helped provide, the nationals spent 2 years cutting all the timber. When Mert and the team arrived, the first pillars were already in the ground, having been carefully set without the benefit of concrete to hold them. Together, Mert, the community, and the U.S. team framed the building and made plans to complete the structure later.*

David: *Vi and I went the following year. We were saddened to learn that much of the beautiful hardwood the locals had previously cut had been sold off by the group downriver that had been hired to store and plane it. With lesser quality supplies we finished the interior and built cabinets. We installed large tanks in the huge crawl space to collect and store fresh roof water that came in torrential downpours. Vi, as main chef for as many as 19 hungry laborers, cooked for the first time with Ecuadorian staples, while resurrecting words from her high school Spanish class to communicate with her helper.*

Phillip: *Thirty years later, people on the river are still getting the care that they need because members of the Corey family, Joyce Bible Church, Redwood Chapel, and Old Cutler Presbyterian Church took teams to help the missionaries. Today members of the next generation are catching the vision to dedicate resources and skills to serve in many parts of the world. At the time of writing, Ron Guderian and his son-in-law, Aleph Fackenthall have recently returned from leading the 13th annual two-week work team to assist native dwellers of the isolated islands of Panama, through water systems, health clinics, teaching, and children's activities.*

[15] A solution used for soaking a person's backside to relieve pain or to aid healing.

[16] Also from Arthur's Dominican Republic journal:

> *We saw brawls on the streets and heard gunshots, and learned that strikes had cancelled flights. One evening we returned to Marilyn's place to the taunts of "Yankee, go home," and a whole spiel of language we couldn't comprehend. I confess it was disconcerting, so I went to the Lord.* REST IN THE LORD AND WAIT PATIENTLY FOR HIM, *took on new meaning. Soon, discord sprung up in the midst of the group and they dispersed. The incident gave me an illustration for my next message...with translation of course. I told how I was slow to give my life to the Lord and how I could not control my temper. I told how God had given me a love for everybody including Dominicans who yelled at me.*
>
> *A few days later, I faced another disparaging encounter. We were giving out Gospel booklets to a group of men in the street when a young ring-leader walked up behind me. Contempt in his voice, he spit out, "Americano!" I paid no heed and continued to hand out pamphlets. Then I walked directly to this person and took him strongly by the shoulders, looked into his eyes and proclaimed, "El Señor le bendiga!" (The Lord bless you). Such boldness surprised those guys. All the men, as well as this fellow, smiled and sent us on our way with blessings.*

[17] Isaac Watts, *Am I a Soldier of the Cross*, 1721, Public Domain.

[18] Using this beast of a vehicle, the author received her driver's license after her first test—a feat not matched by some of her brothers.

[19] Eleanor Phenicie Koon was able to attend Margaret and Arthur's 50th Anniversary celebration at the first family reunion in 1979. After that she moved into Kay's place. She was caring for her sister-in-law fulltime when Margaret passed away in 1990, and was not free to attend her sister's memorial service. When Kay died, Marian and Dennis cleared the place and moved Eleanor to Joyce, to a home assembled right next to Arthur's place. She lived there for a short time before she too died of cancer. Margaret's sister Eleanor left the family a treasure of memories like no other.

[20] Fruit-decorated furniture was inherited by John and Jeanette Corey. The picture went to Janice Lewis. The author later received Naoma's piano. She uses it to teach her own grandchildren.

[21] The author believes Margaret—after taking home the boxes of letters—read through all, but saved only those she wished her children to see.

The archived letters had notations on them in Margaret's handwriting. The years of greatest hardship for Margaret are not represented in the letters that were found after her passing. However, the letters that had been saved gave credence to much of the story contained in this book and in *Sticks, Stones & Songs—The Corey Story.*

[22] John H Sammis, *Trust and Obey,* 1887, Public Domain.

[23] From Arthur's Alaska log:

> The two boys told me they were workers at a church-affiliated youth camp, but neither one professed salvation. We shared a room in a hotel but were ready to leave at 2:15 AM. I turned to the boy who claimed to be atheist. "Of course you don't believe in God, but I do, so I'm going to commit our way to the Lord." At Dawson Creek, I met that boy's parents. I knew God had brought me to minister to this hungry family. When I left their home, the young man pressed $4.00 into my hand and could hardly contain his emotions. God had won—Hallelujah!

[24] Marilyn's injury and care by Joy Wetherald is detailed in *Sticks, Stones & Songs,* p. 24.

[25] In 2018, Pearl Wetherald Nardella discovered the letter Margaret had written on Nov. 17, 1945, to Mabel while she was in the hospital with her newborn, Pearl.

[26] An article in *Port Townsend Leader* on August 7, 2002, reported that a ferry ran from Port Ludlow to Edmonds to Ballard from 1932 to the 1950s.

[27] Axel Fredeen, mentioned in the ferry story, had become a spiritual tower to Arthur in the 1930's—one of his first partners of faith. Axel, like Arthur, knew and quoted the Scripture confidently no matter the situation.

Axel helped cover costs at PBI for the older Corey girls and introduced Arthur to Mike Martin, founder of King's Garden (later Christa ministries) and he too became of prayer friend. Whenever Arthur felt the urge to visit Axel, this co-worker said, "You're the person I asked God to send."

[28] Stuart was paralyzed in a biking accident in 2003. He died in 2006. Laraine lives at their Whidbey home with full-time assistance.

[29] Ray Palmer, *My Faith Looks up to Thee,* 1830, Public Domain.

[30] More details in *Sticks, Stones & Songs.*

[31] McLennans placed a home on the property where Virginia still lives. John McLennan died in 2010.

[32] After the events of 9-11, 2001, Stuart Corey led his Uncle Albert to the Lord. Albert passed away three months later. David Corey has written an account as Stuart reported to him.

[33] Margaret's favorite hymn often flowed from her lips:

--When all my labors and trials are o'er,
and I am safe on that beautiful shore.
Just to be near the dear Lord I adore,
will through the ages be glory for me.

--Friends will be there I have loved long ago.
Joy like a river around me will flow.
Yet just a smile from my Savior, I know,
will through the ages be glory for me.

--Refrain:
Oh, that will be glory for me, glory for me, glory for me,
When by His grace I shall look on His face,
That will be glory, be glory for me.

(Charles H. Gabriel, 1900, Public Domain)

[34] The story of Margaret's passing amidst angelic benediction is recorded in *Sticks, Stones & Songs—The Corey Story,* p. 260. The illness that took her was diagnosed as leiomyoma sarcoma, a cancer that was thought to have originated in her small intestines.

After Margaret's death, Arthur married his widowed sister-in-law, Vera. She became a companion with whom to read the Bible and share the home. Arthur continued his ministry for another handful of years before God took him home on January 25, 1998. His glorious departure for heaven is presented in the epilogue of *Sticks, Stones & Songs.*

ABOUT THE AUTHOR

Eleanor Corey Guderian lives with her husband Ron—less than an hour drive from their three children and families. She holds a BA degree from Seattle Pacific University, an MA from Azusa Pacific University, and a PhD from Walden University. She has authored business workshops and magazine articles, and has earned a Distinguished Toastmaster Award.

After careers in Ecuador and the US as a musician, manager, and consultant, Eleanor became a full-time writer. Her 2014 memoir, *Sticks Stones & Songs—The Corey Story,* portrays life within a spunky, authentic, and imperfect family of twelve in mid-century rural America. She wrote this book, *Pots, Pans & Peace—The Legacy of Margaret Corey,* to tell the rest of the story from her mother's perspective.

Eleanor appreciates hearing from readers of her books. You may contact her at:

Eleanor Corey Guderian
PO Box 571
Stanwood WA 98292

eleanor@eleanorcorey.com
www.eleanorcorey.com

Photo by Aleph Fackenthall

Made in the USA
Columbia, SC
23 February 2020